"ONE CONTINUAL CRY"
David Walker's APPEAL TO THE COLORED CITIZENS OF THE WORLD (1829-1830) : Its Setting, Its Meaning

The American Institute for Marxist Studies (AIMS) is a non-profit educational, research and bibliographical institute. Its purposes are to encourage Marxist and radical scholarship in the United States and to help bring Marxist thought into the forum of reasonable debate to produce a meaningful dialogue among Marxist and non-Marxist scholars and writers. Its policy is to avoid sectarian and dogmatic thinking. It engages in no political activity and takes no stand on political questions. It grinds no axe for any group, party, sect, organization.

To these ends it invites the support and participation of all scholars and public-spirited individuals.

"ONE CONTINUAL CRY"

DAVID WALKER'S APPEAL
TO THE COLORED CITIZENS
OF THE WORLD (1829-1830)

• Walker

Its Setting & Its Meaning
by HERBERT APTHEKER

•

**TOGETHER WITH THE FULL TEXT
OF THE THIRD – AND LAST –
EDITION OF THE *APPEAL***

Published for A.I.M.S. *by*
HUMANITIES PRESS
New York

Library of Congress Catalog Card Number: 65-16703

Type set at The Polyglot Press
Printed in the United States of America

If the abomination were rightly understood, *"one continual cry would be raised in all parts of the confederacy and would cease only with the complete overthrow of the system of slavery, in every part of the country."*
— DAVID WALKER

CONTENTS

INTRODUCTION

MORE than thirteen decades ago, a firebrand was hurled into the charged American air and never has the flame died out.

The governors of slave states convened secret sessions of their legislatures to consider what action this torch—in the guise of a printed work of less than one hundred pages—might require for the better security of "law and order." A frantic correspondence—magistrates to mayors, mayors to governors, governors to Cabinet Members—ensued; draconian laws were enacted; editorials were published; armories were replenished. The land of moonlight, molasses, magnolia and mayhem trembled lest the rattling of the chains—never entirely absent—become so loud as to quite drown out polite conversation about how contented and happy were the you-know-who.

Down through the years this cry from the heart—this *Appeal* from David Walker—has been described in ways as varied as words permit, but dull it has never been called. The slave-holders' newspapers were thrown into paroxysms of rage, of course, at what the *Richmond Enquirer* called this "monstrous slander"—but they never named the awful thing and always referred to it most cryptically lest "the domestics" get wind of it.

A national anti-slavery movement—what is now called the Abolitionist Movement—did not exist when this work appeared; its appearance reflected the jelling, as it simultaneously stimulated the forces that were to constitute that Movement. Outstanding among anti-slavery leaders in this pre-Abolitionist era was the heroic Quaker, Benjamin Lundy, whose peripatetic but marvelously durable paper, *The Genius of Universal Emancipation*, then was being published in Baltimore. In his issue dated April, 1830, Lundy referring to

1

the *Appeal*—by then in its second edition—said, " . . . a more bold, daring, inflammatory publication, perhaps, never issued from the press of any country." But, continued the pacifist, "I can do no less than set the broadest seal of condemnation on it."

William Lloyd Garrison, then Lundy's protege and assistant—a pacifist, though not a Quaker—reacted in a somewhat similar manner; still, Garrison's remarks show deeper insight and brought precious little comfort to slaveowners. It is noteworthy that both Lundy and Garrison permitted some months to go by before they commented on the *Appeal* at all; the first notice taken of it in the *Genius of Universal Emancipation*—written by Garrison—was published January 15, 1830. This was in response to the fact that secret sessions of the Virginia and Georgia State Legislatures had been convened to consider the *Appeal* and that the Governors of both States had expressed the utmost alarm.

Wrote Garrison: "We have had this pamphlet on our table for some time past, and are not surprised at its effect upon our sensitive Southern brethren. It is written by a colored Bostonian and breathes the most impassioned and determined spirit. We deprecate its circulation, though we cannot but wonder at the bravery and intelligence of its author." Garrison returned to Walker's work in a later issue (February 26, 1830) of the same paper; he referred to it "as a most injudicious publication, yet warranted by the creed of an independent people."

Alarm continuing in the slave states and drastic legislative action coming from several of them, Garrison again returned to the *Appeal;* in the issue of March 5, 1830, he stated: "The circulation of this 'seditious' pamphlet has proven one thing conclusively—that the boasted security of the slave States, by their orators and writers, is mere affectation, or something worse." As we shall see, Walker, in the third and final edition of his *Appeal,* made a similar comment.

Among the most influential and militant of the Abolitionists in the generation following Walker's, was the Negro minister, the Rev. Henry Highland Garnet. We shall have occasion later to say more about this remarkable man; here, however, it is noteworthy that his estimate of Walker's *Appeal*, made in 1848, was altogether positive: "The work is valuable, because it is among the first, and was actually the boldest and most direct appeal in behalf of freedom, which was made in the early part of the Anti-Slavery Reformation."

In the post-Civil War generation, when the Civil War Amendments were still taken seriously—prior to the acquiescence in monopoly ownership and Bourbon control of the South that became characteristic from about 1895 to about 1935—one finds Walker's *Appeal* not only mentioned but frequently assessed very highly. This is true, for example, in the memoirs of Abolitionist veterans, as in Samuel J. May's *Some Recollections of the Anti-Slavery Conflict* (Boston, 1868, especially pp. 133-34), and in their biographies, as that of Garrison done by his sons, Francis Jackson and Wendell Phillips Garrison. Here even the limited dissents contemporaneously uttered by the father no longer come from the sons. On the contrary, they describe Walker's effort as being "so original, able and important."*

But with the signing of the "gentlemen's agreement" of 1877, and the sealing of that contract with the blood of thousands of martyrs in the next generation, dominant history writing naturally mirrors—as it bulwarks—dominant interests. In this era, the normal treatment for Walker—as for all Negroes, especially those whose rejection of the status quo is overt—is omission and silence. In the exceptional cases where he is mentioned, as in a Radcliffe College product, we learn that his *Appeal* was "a most bloodthirsty document."**

In the last generation, the worldwide sweep and power of

* *William Lloyd Garrison 1805-1879: The Story of His Life,* told by his children [W. P. and F. J. Garrison] (3 vols., N. Y., 1885, I, p. 159-60).

** Alice D. Adams, *The Neglected Period of Anti-Slavery in America, 1808-1831,* (Boston, 1908, p. 94).

the disinherited—and particularly of the colored peoples of the earth—has made the tactic of silence more and more absurd; hence its practice is tending to disappear. Expressions of hostility, resuscitation of racist notions—in proper "scientific" garb, of course,—and ingenious psychoanalytical explanations for elaborately rephrased chauvinist stereotypes tend now to replace the former coarse slander or gross omission.

The result has been a confrontation of sharp differences of opinion on the work of Walker. Thus, Clement Eaton, who has produced careful studies of the impact of Walker's pamphlet, takes a markedly hostile stance towards its contents— dismissing it as "incendiary" and adding, somewhat gratuitously: "That this publication with its doctrine of servile revolt and its instigation to commit illegal acts deserved suppression hardly admits of a doubt."*

The distinguished scholar and author, J. Saunders Redding, while conveying the passionate quality of the *Appeal*—John Jay Chapman, in his life of *William Lloyd Garrison* (N. Y., 1913) refers to it as "an outcrop of subterranean fire" (p. 51) —nevertheless uses adjectives that do less than justice to the actual content of the work. These are Redding's words:**

> The "Appeal" was not directed to reason although there was reasonable matter in it: it was directed to the passions, in the name of God. Beneath the surface of its religiosity unmeasured doses of poison gave off the odor of sulphur and brimstone. It was scurrilous, ranting, mad—but these were the temper of the times, when nearly every event was climactic and every utterance a shout of rage.

However one may differ from this estimate, one feels that it is based upon a reading of Walker. The same cannot always

* Clement Eaton, *Freedom of Thought in the Old South* (Durham, 1940, pp. 121, 125). See his "A dangerous pamphlet in the Old South," *The Journal of Southern History*, Aug. 1936, II, No. 3, pp. 323-34.

** J. Saunders Redding, *They Came in Chains: Americans from Africa* (Phila. & N. Y., 1950, p. 90).

be said for some excessively brief characterizations that are beginning to appear in the historical literature with the frequency of a cliche. Thus, in Louis Filler's generally able *The Crusade Against Slavery 1830-1860* (N. Y., 1960, p. 23) one finds this sentence: "Walker did not act from a sense of religion, but from a sense of wrong." This is so wide of the mark, that it is a kindness to suggest that its author did not read what he is describing. If there is any one characteristic in the Walker work that is clearer and sharper than any other, it is its religiosity; of course this sense in no way contradicts Walker's equally passionate sense of wrong, rather, it complements and defines it.

The maturing level of the present effort for full equality is perhaps well illustrated in the estimate of Walker's *Appeal* offered by two outstanding historians—one Negro and one white—who have spent decades in the study of slavery in the United States and the effort to abolish it. John Hope Franklin some years ago used words to describe the Walker effort that were markedly similar to those employed over a century ago by Henry Highland Garnet; it was, stated Professor Franklin, "one of the most powerful antislavery tracts written."* Dwight Lowell Dumond, in his *magnum opus, Antislavery: The Crusade for Freedom in America* (Ann Arbor, 1961) calls the *Appeal* "one of the greatest pieces of anti-slavery literature." Professor Dumond offers the opinion, in which the present writer concurs, that: "It was precisely what would have come from a million throats could they have been articulate and have been heard" (p. 329).

To understand Walker's *Appeal* and to comprehend the terrific impact that it had on its own and succeeding generations, it is vital to get some comprehension of the nature of American Negro slavery itself, of the movement to abolish it, and specifically of the decade 1820-1830 at the end of which it burst like a bombshell. Having done these things, one may

* J. H. Franklin, "Slaves Virtually Free in ante-bellum North Carolina," in *The Journal of Negro History*, July, 1943, XXVIII, No. 3, p. 288.

turn properly to a detailed exposition of the particular argument and content of the *Appeal* itself—and then offer its complete text to the reader for his own examination.

Let us turn, then, to each of these tasks; we begin with a brief effort to convey something of the reality of slavery in the United States against which our David hurled his stone.

I: THE SYSTEM OF AMERICAN SLAVERY

For over one hundred and fifty years, the slave-labor of African-derived peoples was a very significant feature of the economy and society of what was to become and did become the United States of America. At the time of the Revolution, out of perhaps three million human beings in the rebellious colonies altogether, some 650,000 were slaves; at the time of the Civil War, out of a total of thirty millions in the nation as a whole, about four millions were slaves—and these, then, were confined south of the Mason-Dixon line. There, in the South, out of a total of some twelve million people, fully one-third were slaves.

For these fifteen or sixteen decades, these slaves produced rice, sugar, indigo, cotton, tobacco, coal, gold, lumber, naval stores, and hemp worth tens of billions of dollars. For this labor they received no wages; from this labor a goodly proportion of the wealth of the United States—and of the world system of capitalism—was derived.

American slavery was a fierce form of tyranny which required and maintained a most ingenious system of control—a system often tested because of the characteristic militancy and discontent of its victims. The basic point to remember is that American slavery was, as Marx stated, "a commercial system of exploitation." That is, American slavery, on the whole, was a staple-producing system dependent upon a world market. There was, therefore, no real limit to the exploiting drive of the slaveowners. And this system was quite as subject to business cycles or periods of so-called prosperity, depression and panic as any other system of private gain dependent upon a world market.

The peculiar feature of this staple-producing system was the fact that the laborers were owned by, were chattels of, the bosses or slaveholders. And the slaveholders, like employers the world over, were in business—that is, ran cotton or sugar or tobacco or rice plantations—for the gain they could derive out of their workers, whom they literally owned. If avarice were not enough, if competition were not enough, if absolute power were not enough, there was the added quality of racism—*i.e.*, the workers so possessed were held to be not really human at all or, at most, innately and significantly and immutably inferior human beings.

Specific factors might worsen the general conditions under which slaves existed. These included depression, soil exhaustion, the expansion of the market. What, however, were those general conditions? The plantation records and journals are perfectly available and quite abundant.

They show: Hours of work were from sun-up to sun-down. Food consisted of corn and occasional meat or fish or molasses.

Slaveholders themselves are the authorities for determining what they spent on their chattels' upkeep. One cotton planter of fifteen years experience, writing in the leading Southern periodical, that published by J. B. DeBow, declared that the masters' expenses were often underestimated. He then proceeded to give what he thought was a proper estimate. The cost of feeding one hundred slaves for one year, he said, was seven hundred and fifty dollars—seven dollars and fifty cents *a year* for each slave's food; and this included, we are told, the expense of the "hospital and the overseer's table." The remaining items—clothing, shoes, bedding, sacks for gathering cotton, and other articles not enumerated—also cost seven dollars and fifty cents per slave per year!

James Madison declared, in 1823, that the annual cost of a slave child in Virginia was from eight to ten dollars, and that the youngster became "gainful to its owner" at about nine years of age. Forty-eight planters of Louisiana informed the U.S. Secretary of the Treasury in 1845 that the yearly expense of supporting the life of a prime field hand was about thirty dollars, and of others—children, aged, some women—fifteen dollars.

A good idea of the habitations of the field hands may be obtained from an article by a Mississippi planter, again in DeBow's publication. The gentleman's purpose in writing the article was to appeal for better slave housing—such as he provided. He owned one hundred and fifty slaves and provided them with twenty-four cabins, each sixteen by eighteen feet. That is, about six slaves "lived" in a hut sixteen by eighteen feet, and this condition was proudly held up for emulation!

Time and again modern readers are assured that cruelty was absent or exceedingly rare in American slavery. The opposite is the truth and the evidence demonstrating this is absolutely overwhelming and easily available. Indeed, it is almost *insulting* to seriously write about such matters; that the myth of idyllic conditions, docile slaves and a placid slave society persists is explicable only as emanating from a deeply chauvinist society, whose existing jim crow order still needs massive doses of demagogy.

The essential point made by those who theorize about the alleged rarity or absence of cruelty in the American slave system revolves around the idea that men would not abuse their own property—in this case, their slaves. Normal people, it is argued, do not maltreat their cows and pianos; then why be cruel to a slave representing a value of several hundred dollars?

It may be noticed, by the way, that present-day society finds it necessary to maintain institutions for the prevention of cruelty to animals and to children, indicating the not infrequent existence of insane, perverse or malicious people. Slave society certainly was conducive to the production of such people.

But, quite apart from this consideration, cruelty was an integral part of the slave system. The argument of interest, as summarized above, might apply, except for two considerations. First—and it is indicative of the nature of the pleaders

9

that this must be pointed out—the slaves were not cows and not pianos. They were, on the contrary, men and women and children. Cows and pianos have never rebelled; the history of Mankind, on the contrary, is the history of repeated human rebellion against injustice and oppression. And, in the second place, the slaves were owned because of their labor power. One may own all the cows in the world—not to speak of pianos —and still starve to death, unless and until human labor power is applied so that one may derive milk or meat.

Slaves were owned in the United States not, essentially, for sexual satisfaction or conspicuous consumption or entertainment—although all three were present; they were owned basically for the profit their owners could derive out of their labor. To obtain that labor, under the given conditions, required guile and deception and force; the last not rarely but regularly employed and continually threatened. This meant cruelty and cruelty was a characteristic and fundamental feature of American Negro slavery.

Documentation for this fills the contemporary sources— diaries, journals, letters, grand jury presentments, newspapers, court records, memoirs. From a myriad of sources, we offer three:

The Grand Jury of Charleston, South Carolina, in 1816, presented "as a most serious evil the many instances of Negro homicides, which have been committed within the city for many years," and went on to refer to "the barbarous treatment of slaves," who were used "worse than beasts of burden."

The British Consul, in the same city, wrote in a personal letter in 1854: "The frightful atrocities of slave holding must be seen to be described. . . . My next door neighbor, a lawyer of the first distinction, and a member of the *Southern Aristocracy,* told me himself that he flogged all his own negroes, men and women, when they misbehaved . . . It is literally no more to kill a slave than to shoot a dog."

Amos Stoddard, a Major in the United States Army, who served many years in the South—especially in Louisiana—wrote of that area in 1811 that, "cruel and even unusual punish-ments are daily inflicted on these wretched creatures, en-feebled, oppressed with hunger, labor and the lash." The Major continued: "The scenes of misery and distress con-stantly witnessed along the coast of the Delta, the wounds and lacerations occasioned by demoralized masters and overseers, most of whom exhibit a strange compound of ignorance and depravity, torture the feelings of the passing stranger, and wring blood from his heart. Good God! why sleeps thy ven-geance!"

Reading such an exclamation from the pen of a U.S. Army Major should make more understandable the call for ven-geance from the pen of David Walker.

While the propaganda mill of the slaveholding oligarchy incessantly ground out its lies about the cowardice and stu-pidity of the Negro and the delights of being a slave, the same group nevertheless maintained a whole series of devices and laws which it knew was necessary to keep the Negro in bondage. That is, the machinery of control was extraordinary, remembering that it was heaven itself that was being regu-lated. This reminds one that fear of the slaves was an ever-present fact in the Old South; the evidence of this is over-whelming. Walker, himself, in the third edition of his pamphlet—as the reader will see further on—commented on the terror that the presence of his work evoked in the South and the inconsistency of such a reaction in the face of the insistence by the rulers of the South as to the contentment that characterized their slaves.

What was the machinery of control? First, the slaveowners owned everything; *i.e.,* if you did not work and work the way you were ordered to, then you would not eat.

Second, the entire legal apparatus was geared to the sanctity not only of property in general but of slave property in par-ticular. Because of this, the law defined the duty and function of the slave, as being absolute submission, while endowing the master with complete power.

11

For actual suppression, armed might was the main reliance. First, most of the U.S. Army was stationed in the South prior to the Civil War. Second, each Southern State had a well-trained and armed militia. Patrols were provided by law for the country-side and these were mounted armed men; in the cities in addition to police there existed special Guards, in some cases—as in Richmond and Charleston—armed with artillery weapons as well as swords, pistols and rifles. Volunteer military organizations abounded in the South, too; the titles of colonel and major proudly borne by the plantation lords were far from simply appellations of courtesy. Furthermore, each master was himself armed and so was the overseer.

The activities of the slaves (and of the free Negroes) were severely limited. None might possess arms. It was illegal to teach a slave to read or write. Writing or saying anything with a "tendency" to create unrest among the slaves was a serious crime. No slave might buy or sell or trade anything without his master's permission. Slaves might not assemble—even for worship—without the presence of whites. They could not testify in any court in any case involving whites.

Numerous non-legal regulations, customs, and mores were important, also, in maintaining subordination. The opinion of a North Carolina judge, rendered in 1852, indicated some of these:

> What acts in a slave towards a white person will amount to insolence, it is manifestly impossible to define—it may consist in a look, the pointing of a finger, a refusal or neglect to step out of the way when a white person is seen to approach. But each of such acts violates the rules of propriety, and if tolerated, would destroy that subordination, upon which our social system rests.

A carefully nursed policy of division between the poor whites and the slaves, on the basis of racism, was another important Bourbon device for retaining his power. Divisions among the slaves, themselves, also were fostered. Thus, the domestic slaves generally were better treated—and often lighter in color—than the field slaves. It was from this favored group that the slaveholders recruited spies and traitors—so excoriated in Walker's *Appeal*—to whom they gave considerable financial rewards together, often, with freedom—the greatest gift in the power of the "patriarchal" slaveholders!

The slaveholders' religion, so far as the slave was concerned, had one message—be meek. In the words of the Rev. Dr. Nelson, who lived for many years in North Carolina:

> I have been intimately acquainted with the religious opportunities of the slaves,—in the constant habit of hearing the sermons which are preached to them. And I solemnly affirm that, during the forty years of my residence and observation in this line, I never heard a single one of these sermons but what was taken up with the obligations and duties of slaves to their masters. Indeed, I never heard a sermon to slaves but what made obedience to masters by the slaves the fundamental and supreme law of religion.

Walker, in his *Appeal*, excoriated the churches for their hypocrisy and their blasphemy in justifying slavery and maintaining a jim crow Christianity. He refers also, as the reader will see, to his own presence in South Carolina at a religious meeting where he was nauseated by the kind of sermon to which the Rev. Dr. Nelson points above. It will not be amiss, therefore, to offer a fairly extensive extract from one such sermon, as published in a book entitled *Sermons Addressed to Masters and Slaves* by the Rev. William Meade, then Bishop of the Episcopal Church in Virginia.*

In the sermon offered by Bishop Meade, slaves are assured that God has willed that they occupy their lowly position. They are told that unless they perform their allotted tasks well they will suffer eternally in Hell. Specifically, they are

* An added connection with Walker is the fact that Meade, when a young Minister in Washington, was a leader in the formation of the American Colonization Society, 1816-17, to which Walker also refers.

warned that the Lord is greatly offended when they are impudent, sullen, stubborn, or disobedient. Nor are they to alter
their behavior if the owner is cross or mean or cruel; that is
the Lord's concern, not theirs, and they are to leave the master's punishment to Him. One fact, particularly—the beatings
and lashings (or, in the sermon's euphonious language, "correction") might make patience difficult. This is recognized,
and explaining it away is done in a most labored and ingenious
manner. The section, though somewhat lengthy is inimitable,
and exact quotation alone does it justice:

There is only one circumstance which may appear grievous
that I shall now take notice of; and this is CORRECTION.
Now, when *correction* is given you, you either deserve it,
or you do not deserve it. But whether you deserve it or not,
it is your duty, and Almighty God requires, that you bear
it patiently.

You may, perhaps, think that this is a hard doctrine; but
if you consider it rightly, you must needs think otherwise
of it. Suppose, then, that you deserve correction; you
cannot but say that it is just and right you should meet
with it. Suppose you do not, or at least you do not deserve
so much or so severe a correction for the fault you have
committed; you perhaps have escaped a great many more,
and are at last paid for all.

Or suppose you are quite innocent of what is laid to your
charge, and suffer wrongfully in that particular thing; is it
not possible you may have done some other bad which was
never discovered, and that Almighty God, who saw you
doing it, would not let you escape without punishment one
time or another? And ought you not in such a case give
glory to Him, and be thankful that He would rather punish
you in this life for your wickedness, than destroy your souls
for it in the next life?

But suppose that even this was not the case—a case hardly
to be imagined—and that you have by no means, known or
unknown, deserved the correction you suffered; there is this
great comfort in it, that if you bear it patiently, and leave

your cause in the hands of God, He will reward you for it in heaven, and the punishment you suffer unjustly shall turn to your exceeding great glory hereafter.

Many slaves—and free Negroes—had a different religion. Their God had declared that all men were created of one blood, and that the divine rule of doing unto others as one would have others do unto you was the true guide for religious behavior. Their God had cursed man-stealers and had himself taken slaves out of their bondage. Their God had denounced the oppressors and had praised the impoverished. Their God had declared that the first would be last and the last would be first. One of the great Prophets of such a God was David Walker.

II: THE ABOLITIONIST MOVEMENT

The goal of the Abolitionist movement in the United States was the elimination of white supremacy, the establishment of full equality for the Negro people. As the first order of business in accomplishing this titanic task, the Abolitionists understood that the system of slavery had to be destroyed; it is often overlooked, however, that the movement itself saw the accomplishment of emancipation as the first giant step towards the aim of destroying racism in the United States.

The Abolitionist crusade has received mainly two forms of treatment in the dominant history-writing. Change has occurred in the past thirty years, but it still remains true that one major mode of approach to this effort is frankly racist, with the authors damning the Abolitionists (white people in every case) as mischievous fanatics, at best. More generally, they are denounced by this school as knaves who attacked with lies and falsehoods a lovely civilization, and who thus "forced" the slaveholders to defend that civilization.

Normally aloof academicians, afflicted with this point of view, come absolutely livid when writing of the Abolitionists. I believe this is due not only to the racism that torments them, but also because they sense the revolutionary nature of that struggle. The Abolitionist movement had as its aim the overthrow of a vested interest representing billions of dollars' worth of private property, and the realization of the Declaration of Independence, with its promise of equality and brotherhood for millions of dark-skinned people whose condition made a mockery of that Declaration.

Such bitterly anti-Abolitionist authors no doubt know that the fight against chattel slavery was a prelude to—and a necessary pre-condition for—the next battle which, in the words of

Wendell Phillips, himself a leading Abolitionist, was to be "that between the working class and the money kings."

The second group writes from a liberal, humanitarian view. They recognize the brutality and ugliness of slavery and so admire those who helped destroy it; but they fail to comprehend the actual nature of the movement and as part of their failure to see this, they fail to consider the vital importance of the Negro people in breaking their own chains, both by independent work and by labor within and through mixed organizations.

Hence, on the whole, when the Abolitionist movement has been dealt with at all sympathetically, the tendency has been to present it as a white person's benevolent association. Negro scholars themselves, notably W.E.B. Du Bois, Carter G. Woodson, and Charles H. Wesley did a great deal to uncover the truth concerning the indispensable role of their forebears in this crusade. Nevertheless, as of this moment their work has not been fully digested within the historical profession and when it comes to the level of ordinary high-school and college instruction and texts, their effort has yet to leave a mark.

Full glory is to be granted to the dauntless white men and women who braved the derision of the press and pulpit, faced the taunts and blows of the "respectable" mobs, tasted the abominations of nineteenth-century prisons, rather than cease the struggle for the liberation of millions of enchained Negroes—and the salvation of the Republic. The reader will note that David Walker in his *Appeal* is generous with his love and praise for the white comrades-in-struggle.

But to overlook or neglect the Negro soldiers in this battle, who filled these prisons; who felt the whip's lash on their backs; built the Underground Railroad and were its passengers; organized societies long before the American Anti-Slavery Society was born, and published anti-slavery newspapers years before *The Liberator* appeared, and made possible by active support and aid both that Society and that newspaper—to "forget" all this is as absurd and erroneous as it would be to

17

"forget" Washington, Jefferson and the Adamses in writing the history of the American Revolution.

Furthermore, to "forget" this is to falsify the Abolitionist movement in a fundamental sense, for it is to fail to understand that this great revolutionary movement—exactly because it was such a movement—was and had to be a Negro-white movement. Any movement in the United States which is not a movement of Negro-white unity is not and cannot be a truly revolutionary one, because one of the fundamental and structural abominations in U.S. society is and has been from its inception, racism.

Cohesiveness, discipline, organization—and correct theory—were vital if the Abolitionist movement were to succeed since it was a revolutionary one. Unless the effort is seen in this light, its character is but dimly grasped, for the Abolitionists set themselves the task of destroying a foul social order, whose roots were deep, whose branches were far spread and whose influence and tenacity were enormous.

Success, it is true—even the partial success that so far has marked the American experience—came and could come only as part of a process of basic socio-economic change; nevertheless, this success was not automatic, it did not come of itself as the spontaneous offshoot of that fundamental change. On the contrary, it was produced by men and women, Negro and white, who had been sowing the seed for decades—talking, writing, petitioning, voting, and who finally piloted an aroused America through the maelstrom of a four-year Civil War. How much work had to be done before the nation willingly set itself the task of excising the cancer of slavery from its vitals; before Lincoln finally would agree that the operation should continue even though as he said, it went on "until all the wealth piled by the bondsman's 250 years of unrequited toil shall be sunk, and until every drop of blood drawn by the lash shall be paid by another drawn by the sword."

To be an Abolitionist was not for the faint-hearted. The slaveholders represented for the first half of the nineteenth century the most closely knit and most important single economic unit in the nation, their millions of bondsmen and millions of acres of land comprising an investment of billions of dollars. This economic might had its counterpart in political power, giving its possessors dominance within the nation and predominance within the South.

And the class-consciousness of this cohesive oligarchy was great. Here are the words of James Hammond, a wealthy slaveholder and leading South Carolina politician. Commenting in 1845 on the bitterness of the exchange between the slaveholders and the Abolitionists, he addressed the latter:

> But if your course was wholly different—if you distilled nectar from your lips and discoursed sweetest music, could you reasonably indulge the hope of accomplishing your object by such means? Nay, supposing that we were all convinced, and thought of slavery precisely as you do, at what era of "moral suasion" do you imagine you could prevail on us to give up a thousand millions of dollars in the value of our slaves, and a thousand millions of dollars more in the depreciation of our lands, in consequence of the want of laborers to cultivate them?

The products wrung from these slaves and this land, made up the blood and bones of the businesses of many of the merchants of the North; many of them, therefore, allied themselves with the Negro's immediate exploiters. Thus it was that a partner in a large New York mercantile house summoned the Reverend Samuel J. May, a leading Abolitionist, one day in 1835, and said:

> Mr. May, we are not such great fools as not to know that slavery is a great evil and a great wrong. But it was consented to by the founders of the Republic. It was provided for in the Constitution of our Union. A great portion of the property of the Southerners is invested under its sanction; and the business of the North as well as of the South, has become adjusted to it.

There are millions upon millions of dollars due from the Southerners to the merchants and mechanics of this city alone, the payment of which would be jeopardized by a rupture between the North and the South. We cannot afford, sir, to let you and your associates succeed in your endeavor to overthrow slavery. It is not a matter of principle with us. It is a matter of business necessity. We cannot afford to let you succeed.

And I have called you out to let you know, that we do not mean to allow you to succeed. We mean, sir, to put you Abolitionists down—by fair means, if we can, by foul means, if we must.

If all this were not enough, the slaveholders did not fail to appreciate, and to point out to the Northern property owners, that the philosophy of Abolitionism—its equalitarianism, its progressivism, and above all, its attack upon the sanctity of private property—represented an ultimate threat to the interests of all possessors. As a Virginian wrote in reply to the questioning of the institution of slavery that flowered following the 1831 insurrection led by Nat Turner:

This one thing we wish to be understood and remembered —that the Constitution of this state, has made Tom, Dick, and Harry, *property*—it has made Polly, Nancy and Molly, *property;* and be that property an evil, a curse, or what not, we intend to hold it. Property, which is considered the most valuable by the owners of it, is a nice thing; and for the right thereto, to be called in question by an unphilosophical set of political mountebanks, under the influence of supernatural agency or deceit, is insufferable.

Somewhat later, John W. Underwood, a wealthy Georgian, warned that the "same torch" which, wielded by the Abolitionists, threatened to consume the fabric of the slave South would, one day, "also cause the northeastern horizon to coruscate with the flames of northern palaces." The essence of the matter was more fully put by a religious and educational leader of South Carolina, Dr. James H. Thornwell, in 1850:

20

The parties in this conflict are not merely Abolitionists and slaveholders—they are atheists, socialists, communists, red republicans, Jacobins on the one side, and the friends of order and regulated freedom on the other. In one word, the world is the battleground—Christianity and atheism the combatants; and the progress of humanity the stake.

The Abolitionists, then, were attacking the lords of the lash who controlled the press and pulpit, who represented "stability" and respectability, and who dominated the political apparatus. To conquer them required wisdom, acute theory, energy, level-headedness and perfect courage, rooted in an overwhelming conviction as to the baseness of slavery. Such courage and conviction would scorn compromise, detest opportunism and would gain strength from the enemy's resistance.

Where would such conviction more surely reside than in the hearts of Negro Americans? Who would better know slavery than those whose backs bore the stripes, into whose eyes had been blazoned the indignities, who had seen their own children or their own parents sold like hogs?

Facts and considerations such as these must be kept in mind when one reads so impassioned a document as Walker's *Appeal*.

* * *

The Abolitionist effort was permeated by three major schools of thought; one held that the only proper and effective instrument for change was moral suasion; another held that moral suasion had to be buttressed by political action; the third expressed a belief in the necessity for resistance in a physical sense, in direct, militant action. Members of the last school adopted, at times, the methods of the first two as well. A major division of opinion—as between Frederick Douglass and Henry Highland Garnet, for example—did not revolve around the justice of militant resistance. Rather, it revolved around the question of the *strategy*—not so much the tactic—of the battle to end slavery. Douglass did not denounce those slaves who—finding no means of resistance open to them and being driven to despair—resorted to or planned to resort to insurrection; on the contrary, he expressed his sympathy for and support of their heroic efforts. What Douglass did hold, however, was that what was required to abolish slavery in the United States was the *revolutionising of its politics,* and that this required careful, concerted political action and struggle. Douglass insisted that only this—given all the circumstances in the United States where, unlike Haiti, the slaves formed ten percent, rather than ninety percent of the population—could lead to the emancipation of the slaves.

The Negro people as a whole—and the Abolitionist movement as a whole—adopted that strategy. This does not mean, however, that the Negro people—or the Abolitionist movement generally—were pacifists; on the contrary, in the vast majority they, and it, adopted the view of the Declaration of Independence and held that forcible repression and violent tyranny did justify forcible resistance thereto.

Among the earliest protests against American slavery may be found the kernel of this militancy: the righteousness of the cause for which slaves conspired and fought was acknowledged. In the famous Germantown Quaker Protest against slavery of 1688, the authors put this question: Suppose the slaves rebel here and now, as they frequently have done elsewhere at other times, "will these masters and mastrisses take the sword at hand and warr against these poor slaves, licke, we are able to believe, some will not refuse to doe; or have these negers not as much right to fight for their freedom, as you have to keep them slaves?" Ten years later, again in Pennsylvania, another Quaker protest against slavery, signed by Robert Pyle, asked a similar question: Suppose our slaves do rebel, and blood is shed? The Friend wondered, "whether our blood will cry innocent whether it will not be said you might have let them alone."

The Grand Jury of Charles Town, South Carolina, made the following interesting charge in March, 1741:

> We present as a Public Grievance a certain book or Journal sign'd by Hugh Brian, directed to ye Honble, the Speaker, and the rest of the members of the Commons house Assembly in Charles Town, which we have perused and find in general, contains sundry enthusiastic Prophecys, of the destruction of Charles Town, and deliverance of the Negroes from their Servitude, and that by the Influence of ye said Hugh Brian, great bodys of Negroes have assembled to gether on pretence of religious worship, Contrary to ye laws, and destructive of ye Peace . . .

Other whites, Jonathan Brian, William Gilbert, and Robert Ogle, also were declared to possess opinions inimical to the security of a slave society. Mr. Brian's work was suppressed, but what punishment, if any, was meted out to the individuals is not known.

Some of the literature produced just before and during the Revolutionary War contained, as one might expect, passages justifying—if not actually urging—attempts on the part of the slaves to achieve their freedom through rebellion. The writings of James Otis,* for example, particularly his famous pamphlet published in Boston in 1764, *The Rights of the British Colonies Asserted and Proved,* excoriated the institution of slavery, and affirmed the Negro's inalienable right to freedom. The logical deduction was plain, and did not pass unnoticed, as John Adams testified:

> Young as I was, and ignorant as I was, I shuddered at the doctrine he taught and I have all my life shuddered, and still shudder, at the consequence that may be drawn from such premises. Shall we say, that the rights of masters and

---

* There is special irony to the fact that James Otis wrote what he did about Negro slavery, for his direct descendant, Harrison Gray Otis, was Mayor of Boston when Walker published his *Appeal*—a work that horrified the Revolutionist's grandson, though, it must be stated, the Mayor refused the request from Georgia to suppress the book.

23

servants clash, and can be decided only by force? I adore the ideal of gradual abolitions.. But who shall decide how fast or how slowly these abolitions shall be made?

Mrs. John Adams, on the other hand—the redoubtable Abigail—wrote to her husband in September, 1774, then busily leading a revolutionary effort in Philadelphia, of the discovery of a fairly widespread plot to rebel among slaves in and around Boston: "I wish most sincerely there was not a slave in the province; it always appeared a most iniquitous scheme to me to fight ourselves for what we are daily robbing and plundering from those who have as good a right to freedom as we have."

Another popular pamphlet of the pre-Revolutionary period, that by the Reverend Isaac Skillman, *An Oration upon the Beauties of Liberty, or the Essential Rights of the Americans* (published in Boston in 1772 and in its fourth printing by 1773), vehemently attacked the enslavement of the Negroes, demanded their immediate liberation, and affirmed: "Shall a man be deem'd a rebel that support his own rights? It is the first law of nature, and he must be a rebel to God, to the laws of nature, and his own conscience, who will not do it." Very much the same point was made by the Reverend Samuel Hopkins, of Newport, Rhode Island, in a work first published in 1776.

The essence of this is repeated by James Madison in 1783, in a letter commenting upon one of his own slaves who had fled and been captured. "I cannot think of punishing him," wrote the future President, "by transportation [that is, by sale into West Indian slavery] merely for coveting that liberty for which we have paid the price of so much blood, and have proclaimed so often to be the right, & worthy the pursuit of every human being."

From the time of the Revolution on, the action of the colonists was often referred to by militant Abolitionists publicly—and not merely in private by troubled slaveowners, as

Mr. Madison—in order to support their own views justifying slave rebellion. One of the earliest writings of this kind was signed "Free Negro" and appeared in 1789 in the leading magazine of the time—*The American Museum,* published in Philadelphia. This anonymous Negro author denounced slavery, denied the oft-repeated idea of his people's "inferiority," and demanded: "Do the rights of nature cease to be such, when a Negro is to enjoy them? Or does patriotism, in the heart of an African, rankle into treason?"

In this same period Thomas Paine wrote from Paris to an anonymous friend in Philadelphia concerning anti-slavery efforts then in progress. His concluding remarks were: "We must push this matter [Negro slavery] further on your side of the water. I wish that a few well instructed could be sent among their brethren in bondage; for until they are enabled to take their own part, nothing will be done."

A physician, Dr. George Buchanan, delivered a very militant speech on July 4, 1791, before a public meeting of the Maryland Society for Promoting the Abolition of Slavery. In the course of it occur these passages, spoken six weeks before the outbreak of the great Haitian Revolution:

> What then, if the fire of Liberty shall be kindled amongst them? What, if some enthusiast in their cause shall beat to arms, and call them to the standard of freedom? Would they fly in clouds, until their numbers became tremendous, and threaten the country with devastation and ruin? . . .
>
> Led on by hopes of freedom, animated by the aspiring voice of their leader, they would soon find, that "a day, an hour of virtuous liberty, was worth a whole eternity of bondage."

With the eruption of the Haitian Revolution, many people felt called upon to declare their attitudes towards it, and some, who gloried in the French and American Revolutions, found it but consistent and logical to welcome that which occurred in the West Indies. Typical was the Bostonian, J. P.

Martin, who wrote in an article entitled, "Rights of Black Men," and published in *The American Museum* in 1791:

> We believe that freedom is the natural right of all rational beings, and we know that the blacks have never voluntarily resigned that freedom. Then is not their cause as just as ours? . . . Let us be consistent, Americans, if we justify our own conduct in the late glorious revolution, let us justify those who, in a cause like ours, fight with equal bravery.

A delegate to the Kentucky Constitutional Convention of 1792, the Reverend David Rice—known as the father of Presbyterianism in that State—argued against the establishment of slavery, declaring it to be "a perpetual war, with an avowed purpose of never making peace," and an institution that would weaken the home front and strengthen an enemy. He pointed to the events then transpiring in the West Indies, and declared: "There you may see the sable, let me say the brave sons of Africa, engaged in a noble conflict with their inveterate foes. There you may see thousands fired with a generous resentment of the greatest injuries, and bravely sacrificing their lives on the altar of liberty."

A very prominent resident of Connecticut—later to be a Congressman—Theodore Dwight, went even further in a public address delivered two years later before the state Society for the Promotion of Freedom. Here he applied the case right to the United States. Warning of coming plots and uprisings, he continued:

> And when hostilities are commenced, where will they [the slaveholders] look for auxiliaries, in such an iniquitous warfare? Surely, no friend to freedom and justice will dare to lend them his aid . . . Who then can charge the negroes with injustice, or cruelty, when they "rise in all vigour of insulted nature," and avenge their wrongs. What American will not admire their exertions, to accomplish their own deliverance?

26

Like sentiments occasionally were published in the press, as in the *Hartford Courant* in 1796 and 1797. In the latter year, too, the Massachusetts Negro leader, Prince Hall—a veteran of the Revolutionary War, a fighter against slavery, a prominent figure in the Masonic movement—expressed admiration for the activities of his brothers in Haiti.

Early in 1804, a judge of the eastern district of Georgia, Jabez Brown, Jr., created a sensation by his "inflammatory" charge to the grand jury of Chatham. The jury refused to permit the publication of the charge and bitterly denounced the judge. Other evidence makes clear that the judge had criticized slavery in the most severe terms, even stating that he thought rebellion by the slaves fully justifiable. This remarkable Georgia judge actually was briefly jailed for "inciting insurrection"; he later was released and in effect exiled to Rhode Island.

In Howard County, Missouri, in 1819, a grand jury indicted a white man named Humphrey Smith on the grounds that his remarks were inciting slave rebellion, but the outcome of this case is not known. In October, 1822, four white men were arrested and convicted of having encouraged the slaves involved in the Vesey plot. These Charlestonians were Andrew S. Rhodes, of English descent; William Allen, Scottish; Jacob Danders, German; and John Igneshias, Spanish. Only Allen's motives were suspect since a free Negro charged that he had expected to reap financial gain from successful rebels. The others, however, hated slavery, and their crime consisted in letting the Negroes know this and in telling them, as the German put it, "they had as much right to fight for their liberty as the white people." All were sentenced to prison terms ranging from three to twelve months and to fines from one hundred to one thousand dollars, which had to be paid before release from jail.

In the year 1829, three works appeared produced by Negroes which contained more or less open calls for, or justification of, rebellion. The least clear of these is the remarkable book of

27

poems, called *The Hope of Liberty*, written by George Moses Horton, a slave of Chatham County, North Carolina, and published originally by Joseph Gales, editor of a leading newspaper, the *Raleigh Register*. Occasional lines were quite militant; for example:

> Oh, Liberty, thou golden prize
>   So often sought by blood—
> We crave thy sacred sun to rise,
>   The gift of Nature's God!
> Bid slavery hide her haggard face,
>   And barbarism fly:
> I scorn to see the sad disgrace
>   In which enslaved I lie.

Money was raised, largely in free Negro communities in the North, to purchase the freedom of Horton. One of those who participated in this successful effort was David Walker.

A truculent note of foreboding and militance was struck by the rather strange and mystical pamphlet issued in New York City by a free Negro, Robert Alexander Young. This is called *The Ethiopian Manifesto Issued in Defence of the Black Man's Rights, in the Scale of Universal Freedom*. Notable here was the prophecy of the coming of a Negro savior who, being invincible, will lead his people to freedom; there is a hint of this also—and quite independently—in Walker's work. And that is the third to appear in the year 1829 from Negroes and carrying fervently the message of freedom. To know this, and to know something of the nature of the whole struggle against slavery and, in particular, the developing idea of militant resistance thereto is to be in a better position to comprehend Walker and his *Appeal*.

Let us now turn more specifically to the decade 1820-1830, within which Walker's work appears.

III: THE WATERSHED: 1820-1830

Wherever there has been slavery—and no part of the world has been wholly without it—there has been anti-slavery feeling; in the first place, the feeling appeared among the slaves but more or less quickly and more or less deeply, it appeared among non-slaves, too.

Certainly, this was true of the United States. Before the founding of the Republic, and in its very first years, distinguished figures like Anthony Benezet, Benjamin Rush, Benjamin Franklin, Thomas Paine, John Jay had not only spoken out against slavery but had taken organizational steps of an emancipationist nature.

American Negroes expressed themselves, also, not only in the activities of the hundreds of thousands in slavery, but also in the writings and work of those tens of thousands who were free. Men like Prince Hall, Benjamin Banneker, Absalom Jones, and Richard Allen published pamphlets prior to the 19th century in which appeared very nearly every argument to be developed in the later and more national Abolitionist movement. Their writings in particular attacked the concept of racial inferiority, denied the alleged docility of the slaves, and warned that the longer the evil of slavery persisted, the more costly and catastrophic would be its inevitable destruction.

The beginnings of Negro organization likewise go back to these years, and no matter what the ostensible purpose of these groups were—religious, philanthropic, or literary—the very act on the part of oppressed people of joining together was itself revolutionary; moreover, all of them, sooner or later, in fact explicitly became part of the anti-slavery crusade.

Thus, in the spring of 1787, Philadelphia Negroes, including Richard Allen, Absalom Jones, William White, Mark Stevenson, William Gray, and others, formed a Free African Society whose original stated purpose was largely convivial, but by 1790 it was devoting itself to anti-slavery agitation, the prevention of Negro kidnapping, and cooperation with other emancipationist groups, such as State manumission societies and Quakers. Shortly afterward, Henry Stewart, a member of the Philadelphia society, moved to Newport, Rhode Island, and established a similar association there. Another such group was formed in New York City in 1795, and within three years still another African Society was created in Boston. From these societies came the inspiration for public meetings, petitions, pamphlets, and conferences all devoted to attacking slavery.

The first generation of the nineteenth century witnessed a significant expansion in anti-slavery activities, notably in several Southern States. Among white people in the early 19th century who were notable in this regard were Charles Osborn, Elihu Embree, William Swaim and Benjamin Lundy. Concern about slavery grew among Quakers, and the feeling that the Society of Friends as a whole was too passive in the face of this abomination helped lead in 1825 to the Hicksite split-off, led by the fierce anti-slavery battler, Elias Hicks.

With the admission of Missouri as a slave state in 1820, and the so-called Compromise of that date, which legalized the existence of the monstrosity south of the 36°30' latitude, the intense pre-occupation politically with the slave question started. It is the debate around this legislation that Jefferson characterized as a "fire-bell in the night." While the powers-that-be decreed that this settlement was to be considered definitive and that from thence onward the "question" was out of bounds for polite conversation, Jefferson was writing in a letter to a friend, April 13, 1820: "But this is a reprieve only, not a final sentence. I have been among the most sanguine in believing that our Union would be of long duration. I now doubt it very much."

30

As anti-slavery activities among white people actually intensified prior to and after this Compromise, so did it among Negroes. Among the individuals who stand out during this formative period was Peter Williams, Jr., a minister in New York City, whose efforts to arouse his countrymen to the iniquities of slavery attracted attention as early as 1806. His work in this field continued for thirty years and led to his appointment in 1834 to the Board of Managers of the pioneering American Anti-Slavery Society. Events such as large-scale meetings of Negro men and women occurred in 1807 and 1808 in various Northern cities, notably Philadelphia and New York, celebrating the passage of the federal anti-slave trade law and contributing towards publicizing the cause of freedom.

A few years later another Negro whose career was to continue on into the 1830's, James Forten of Philadelphia, made himself felt on behalf of his people's liberation. He gained notice particularly in 1813 by his vigorous denunciation of projected jim crow regulations in Pennsylvania, and in 1817, together with Russell Parrott, was important in bringing together three thousand Philadelphia Negroes. These people went on record as being decidedly opposed to the purposes of the recently launched American Colonization Society; they announced their determination to win justice for themselves and their enslaved brethren in their native land, rather than to seek a dubious refuge elsewhere and so withdraw from the struggle for the slaves' emancipation. In the words of the assembled thousands—words to be echoed in the impassioned prose of David Walker:

> Let not a purpose be assisted which will stay the cause of the entire abolition of slavery in the United States, and which may defeat it altogether; which proffers to those who do not ask for them *benefits,* but which they consider *injuries,* and which must insure to the multitudes, whose prayers can only reach through us, *misery, sufferings, and perpetual slavery.*

31

It will help in understanding the concentration upon colonization as a foe of the anti-slavery effort—which forms one of the main themes in Walker's *Appeal*—to observe that at the founding meeting of the American Colonization Society, held in Washington in December, 1816, the presiding officer was Henry Clay, himself—he had already been a U.S. Senator and was at that moment Speaker of the House. Among the twenty founding members of the Society was the leading Virginia politician, John Randolph, several Lees of Virginia including one who at the moment was the Mayor of Alexandria, a Senator and a Congressman from Maryland, a U.S. General, the Clerk of the House, and several Ministers, including William Meade—whom we already met. Two of the inspirers of the Society were Elias B. Caldwell, mentioned by Walker, who was, and had been for many years, Chief Clerk of the U.S. Supreme Court, and the wealthy attorney—and song-writer— Francis Scott Key.*

With such backing, it will be understood that this Society was a thoroughly respectable, and quite influential, one. After the Missouri Compromise it was meant to help secure physical quiet to encase the political quiet that had been decreed by that piece of legislation. By 1825 there appeared in Washington the monthly organ of this Society; it was called *African Repository and Colonial Journal*—it lasted until 1892! —and it is to this that Walker refers and from this that he occasionally quotes.

In the 1820's the States of Maryland and Virginia appropriated rather modest sums to assist the Colonization Society; by 1832 the Legislatures of Ohio, Indiana, Pennsylvania, Massachusetts, Maryland, Kentucky, and New York had

* One of the books mentioned by Walker is by a physician, Jesse Torrey, *A Portraiture of Domestic Slavery in the United States* . . . (Phila. 1817). Torrey had gone to Washington in 1816 in an effort to save several free Negroes who had been kidnapped. His effort failed but the attorney who served Torrey was—Francis Scott Key!

memorialized Congress in favor of federal aid to the Society, though this never actually materialized.

Simultaneously, however, as has been stated, anti-slavery agitation and organization intensified. Notable was the fact that the Vermont legislature, in 1826, sent a resolution to that of North Carolina, stating that "slavery is an evil to be deprecated by a free and enlightened people," and offering to cooperate "in any measures which may be adopted by the general government for its abolition in the United States." North Carolina's response, after spurning Vermont's suggestion, was to tighten, in 1827, its slave-patrol and militia laws.

On the other hand, in 1827, the New York law abolishing all slavery within its boundaries went into effect; this naturally stimulated the entire abolitionist effort and was the occasion for many mass meetings and messages of congratulations. Influential, also, was the rapid growth in the anti-slavery movement in Great Britain—to result in 1833, in the gradual emancipation of slaves in the British West Indies. It was this, plus the fact that Canada was more and more openly serving as a haven for runaway slaves,* that no doubt accounts for Walker's laudatory references to the English.

The 1820's also is one of the periods of most intense slave unrest. This is to be seen in the context of world-wide democratic and militant awakenings. In the United States, it is the period of the Jacksonian triumph and the lusty beginnings of a politically conscious labor movement. Revolutionary outbreaks of major proportions occurred also in Spain— these efforts and their repression are several times noticed by Walker—Turkey, Greece, Italy, France, Belgium, Poland, South America, Mexico and the West Indies. The last directly involved slaves, while in South America and Mexico the upheavals resulted in furthering the anti-slavery cause (Mexico

* In the 1820's, Clay as Secretary of State tried to get Canada to agree to the return of runaway slaves; he was not successful. This also is referred to by Walker.

abolished slavery in 1829). These developments created concern among Southern slaveowners. Another source of worry for them was the attempt made during this period by Mexico and Colombia, apparently backed by England and France, to get rid of slavery and of Spanish rule in Cuba and Puerto Rico.

Serious insurrections among slaves occurred during the 1820's in Martinique, Puerto Rico, Cuba, Antigua, Tortola, Demerara, and Jamaica. News of them regularly appeared in the press of the United States, particularly outside of the South.

Certain it is that the activity of maroons—outlying, pugnacious fugitive slaves within the South—increased in the 1820's. Several southern cities suffered from slave-set fires, notably Petersburg, Virginia, Mobile, Alabama, and Augusta, Georgia; uprisings aboard domestic slave-trading vessels recurred and two, in 1826, actually succeeded and created something of a sensation. Plots were very numerous, and some, as that led by Denmark Vesey in Charleston in 1822, involved thousands of slaves.

One of the instances of slave militancy is specifically referred to—and briefly described—in Walker's *Appeal*. Bearing in mind that this is but one episode in dozens that constantly rocked the slaveholders' society in this decade, it will not be out of order to describe this particular one in some detail.* Since it occurred in August, it was reported in newspapers later that month and early in September (for example, in the *Southern Advocate,* Huntsville, Ala., August 22, 1829; *Niles' Weekly Register* (Baltimore), September 5, 1829) and was read by Walker while he was composing his *Appeal.*

One August morning in 1829, two male slaves in a coffle of ninety men, women and children—recently bought in Maryland and being led South for sale—suddenly dropped their

---

* Full details on the slave unrest of the 1820's will be found in the present writer's *American Negro Slave Revolts* (N. Y., 1943; new edition, 1963), chapter XI.

shackles, at a point between Greenup and Vanceburg, Kentucky, and began to deal blows upon one another. William B. Petit, one of the three white men leading and guarding this valuable group of humans, rushed up at them with his whip, ordering them to fall back into line.

Instantly it became clear that, in some way, the shackles on each of the men had been filed through; they set upon and killed Mr. Petit. Another of the guards, Gabriel T. Allen, coming to the latter's aid, was also killed, and the owner, a well-known slave trader named Henry Gordon, then was attacked. He, however, with the assistance of a slave woman, managed to mount a horse and, though pursued by one of the rebels, made good his getaway and rounded up assistance.

The posse thus formed succeeded in capturing all the slaves; six of their leaders—five men and one woman—were sentenced to hang. The woman was found to be pregnant and permitted to remain in jail for several months until after the birth of her child, whereupon, on May 25, 1830, she was publicly executed. The men were hanged November 20, 1829. The next day, the Portsmouth, Virginia *Times,* declared that "they all maintained to the last, the utmost firmness and resignation to their fate. They severally addressed the assembled multitude, in which they attempted to justify the deed they had committed." According to the well-known Baltimore paper, *Niles' Weekly Register,* December 26, 1829, one of the condemned Negroes, "the instant before he was launched from the cart, exclaimed, 'Death—death at any time in preference to slavery.' "

It is as though this martyr had read Walker's *Appeal.*

In the 1820's several additional Negro leaders of great force came forward. These included the Reverend Nathaniel Paul of Albany, New York, the Reverend John Gloucester and William Whipper of Philadelphia, William J. Watkins and Hezekiah Grice* of Baltimore, Lewis Woodson and John

* Walker, in his *Appeal,* refers to "our colored Baltimorean." It is almost

Peck of Pittsburgh, Austin Steward of Rochester, and many others, as Christopher Rush, Philip A. Bell, Samuel E. Cornish, Peter Williams, William Hamilton, and Frederick Hinton. From them appeared new societies to join those already named, such as the General Colored Association of Massachusetts, the African Baptist Society of Albany, the African Clarkson Society of New York (named in honor of Thomas Clarkson, a pioneer anti-slavery leader in England), and the Reading Room Society in Philadelphia.

Thus it was that by the time the national anti-slavery organizations were formed in the 1830's, there already existed about fifty such Negro groups spread throughout the country, having valuable experience and most eager to join forces with the newcomers.

The cause had developed sufficiently among the Negro people, in fact, for them to be able to create and to support a weekly organ devoted to its enhancement. On March 16, 1827, *Freedom's Journal,* owned and edited by Samuel E. Cornish and John B. Russwurm, made its appearance in New York City. Before this journal terminated its existence in 1829—hastened in part by the renegacy of Russwurm and his affiliation with the American Colonization Society—it had secured agents throughout New England, New York, Pennsylvania, Maryland, the District of Columbia, and even in Virginia and North Carolina, as well as in Haiti, Canada and England.

One of the staunch organizers of and lecturers for the Colored Association of Massachusetts was David Walker. An original subscriber to *Freedom's Journal* was David Walker; he was an agent for the paper in Boston, contributed to it occasionally, and regularly advertised his clothing store—located on Brattle Street—in its pages. He was also, as one may read in his *Appeal,* a strong supporter of the paper that

---

certain he has in mind Grice, who was the main spirit behind the launching of the First National Convention of Colored People, in 1830. On this, see my *Documentary History of the Negro People in the U.S.* (N.Y., new edition, 2 vols. 1962, 1964) I, pp. 98-107.

Samuel E. Cornish founded two months after the closing of *Freedom's Journal*. This new paper, also issued in New York City, was called *Rights of All;* its first number appeared May 29, 1829 and its sixth—and final number—October 9, 1829.

With the development of sharpened conflict over the slavery question in the 1820's, there developed also significant defenses of the institution in the South. Basic to this was the revitalization of racism, and bestial displays of this poison in the form of lynchings and vigilante-style assaults upon Negro ghettoes.

Related to all this were developments in Ohio, to which Walker refers more than once in his *Appeal;* elucidation of this in particular will therefore be pertinent.

By 1829, about 2,200 Negroes lived in Cincinnati, many of them fugitives from the South. That year city authorities by proclamation demanded that all Negroes obey, within sixty days, an Ohio law of 1807, hitherto dormant, requiring the registration and bonding, in the sum of $500, of every Negro. The Negroes in mass meeting requested an additional thirty days and sent a delegation to Canada to prepare for migration. The time extension was not granted, and a mob attacked the Negro area for three days. The Negroes fought back and finally drove the mob away. When the Canadian delegation returned with a favorable report, about one thousand Negroes left Cincinnati and established Wilberforce Settlement, near London, Ontario.

IV: GARNET ON WALKER

Henry Highland Garnet, minister, newspaper editor, fighter for freedom, was born a slave in New Market, Maryland in 1815. As a mere child of nine, he managed to escape and made his way to New York City. He entered a school maintained in the city by Negro men and women. In 1834, he was a leader of 150 Negro youth, below the age of 20, who founded The Garrison Literary and Benevolent Association in New York. It is worth noting that at their founding meeting, these youth gathered in a public school but a city official told them they would have to change the name of their society if they wished to continue using public facilities. They retained the name and obtained different quarters.

In 1835 Garnet was invited to attend an academy in Canaan, New Hampshire, but the building was destroyed by a mob enraged that a Negro had been asked to be a student there. He was befriended by the anti-slavery minister, Beriah Green, and his ministerial education was continued under his guidance at Oneida Institute in Whitestown, New York—which, despite its name, tolerated the colored scholar!

The magnificent Negro orator and minister, the Rev. Theodore S. Wright, also helped forward his education. Through the 1840's he served as a minister in Troy, New York, later for a short time he worked in Jamaica, West Indies, and still later took over the pastorate of the Shiloh Presbyterian Church in New York City when Mr. Wright died. He was an active supporter of the Union cause during the Civil War and in 1864 became a pastor in Washington. In 1865, at the request of the House of Representatives, he preached in Congress a sermon celebrating the enactment of the Thirteenth Amendment. Towards the close of his life, Garnet was appointed U.S. Minister to Liberia; he died there at his post on February 13, 1882.

Walker's thinking, as expressed in his *Appeal,* had a decisive effect upon the thinking and the life of Garnet. This manifested itself especially beginning in 1843. In that year, August 21-24, a National Negro Convention was held in Buffalo, New York. Over seventy delegates from a dozen States were present, including such young and rising figures as Frederick Douglass, William Wells Brown, Charles B. Ray, Charles L. Remond, and Garnet.

At this Convention Garnet delivered a very militant speech, entitled "An Address to the Slaves of the United States," which attracted national attention and which failed by one vote of being adopted as the sentiments of the convention. The deep imprint of Walker is clear. The essence of this essay of about 4,000 words is conveyed in this extract:*

> Inform them [the slaveholders, Garnet meant, directing himself to the slaves] that all you desire is FREEDOM, and that nothing else will suffice. Do this, and for ever after cease to toil for the heartless tyrants, who give you no other reward but stripes and abuse. If they then commence the work of death, they, and not you, will be responsible for the consequences. You had better die—*die immediately,* than live slaves and entail your wretchedness upon your posterity. If you would be free in this generation, here is your only hope. However much you and all of us may desire it, there is not much hope of redemption without the shedding of blood. If you must bleed, let it all come at once—rather *die freemen, than live to be slaves.*

In 1848, Garnet produced a volume containing the text of the *Appeal* by Walker, a sketch of Walker's life and the text of his own 1843 address; there is some evidence that part of the money for the publication of this volume was supplied by an up-State farmer, not yet very well known, called John Brown.

* For the entire text, see my *Documentary History of the Negro People in the United States,* I, pp. 226-233.

In 1849 the State Convention of Colored Citizens of Ohio passed a resolution authorizing the purchase and gratuitous distribution of five hundred copies of this 1848 Garnet work; whether or not this was actually done is not known. Certainly, today, the Garnet volume is exceedingly rare.*

Because of its rarity and because it is the fullest work directly dealing with the life of David Walker, that section of it which is biographical is herewith reproduced in its entirety.

There is, first of all, a two paragraph preface, dated Troy, New York, April 12, 1848, which reads as follows:

> Such is the very high esteem which is entertained for the memory of David Walker, and so general is the desire to preserve his "Appeal," that the subscriber has undertaken and performed the task of re-publication, with a brief notice of his life, having procured permission from his widow, Mrs. Dewson.
>
> The work is valuable, because it was among the first, and was actually the boldest and most direct appeal in behalf of freedom, which was made in the early part of the Anti-Slavery Reformation. When the history of emancipation of the bondmen of America shall be written, whatever name shall be placed first on the list of heroes, that of the author of the Appeal will not be second.

Then follows a section of Garnet's work which is entitled;

A BRIEF SKETCH
of the
LIFE AND CHARACTER OF DAVID WALKER

---

* *Walker's Appeal, with a brief sketch of his life,* by Henry Highland Garnet, *and also Garnet's Address to the Slaves of the United States* (N. Y., 1848, J. H. Tobitt). This work is as rare as the original Walker pamphlet; the copy that had been in the Schomburg Collection of the N. Y. Public Library is now missing. That collection does have, however, a photostatic reproduction of Garnet's "Sketch" of Walker's Life. Garnet's own 1843 Address was republished, along with his *Memorial Discourse* before Congress in 1865, by James McCune Smith, in Philadelphia in the latter year.

And here is the text of that section, in full:

It is generally the desire of the reader of any intellectual production, to know something of the character and life of the author. The character of *David Walker* is indicated in his writings. In regard to his life, but a few materials can be gathered; but what is known of him, furnishes proof to the opinion which the friends of man have formed of him—that he possessed a noble and courageous spirit, and that he was ardently attached to the cause of liberty.

Mr. Walker was born in Wilmington, North Carolina, Sept. 28, 1785. His mother was a free woman, and his father was a slave.* His innate hatred to slavery was very early developed. When yet a boy, he declared that the slaveholding South was not the place for him. His soul became so indignant at the wrongs which his father and kindred bore, that he determined to find some portion of his country where he would see less to harrow his soul. Said he, 'If I remain in this bloody land, I will not live long. As true as God reigns, I will be avenged for the sorrow which my people have suffered. This is not the place for me—no, no. I must leave this part of the country. It will be a great trial for me to live on the same soil where so many men are in slavery; certainly I cannot remain where I must hear their chains continually, and where I must encounter the insults of their hypocritical enslavers. Go, I must.'

The youthful Walker embraced his mother, and received a mother's blessings, and turned his back upon North Carolina. His father died a few months before his birth; and it is a remarkable coincidence that the son of the subject of this Memoir, was a posthumous child.**

After leaving home, David Walker travelled rapidly

---

* In accordance with the law in the slave States, therefore, David Walker was born free, since for Negroes—unlike whites—the law stated that their own condition would follow that of the mother, not of the father. Generally, of course, where the parents were slave and free, the mother was a slave and the father was a white man, often a slaveowner, who, thus, in accordance with law, had both pleasure and profit.

** This was Edwin G. Walker, who in 1866 became the first Negro elected to the State Legislature of Massachusetts.

towards the North, shaking off the dust of his feet, and breathing curses upon the system of human slavery,* America's darling institution. As might be expected he met with trials during his journey; and at last he reached Boston, Mass., where he took up his permanent residence. There he applied himself to study, and soon learned to read and write, in order that he might contribute something to the cause of humanity. Mr. Walker, like most of reformers, was a poor man—he lived poor, and died poor.

In 1827 he entered into the clothing business in Brattle street, in which he prospered; and had it not been for his great liberality and hospitality, he would have become wealthy. In 1828, he married Miss Eliza—.** He was emphatically a self-made man, and he spent all his leisure moments in the cultivation of his mind. Before the Anti-Slavery Reformation had assumed a form, he was ardently engaged in the work. His hands were always open to contribute to the wants of the fugitive. His house was the shelter and the home of the poor and needy. Mr. Walker is known principally by his "Appeal," but it was in his private walks, and by his unceasing labors in the cause of freedom, that he has made his memory sacred.

With an overflowing heart, he published his "Appeal" in 1829. This little book produced more commotion amongst slaveholders than any volume of its size that was ever issued from an American press. They saw that it was a bold attack upon their idolatry, and that too by a black man who once lived among them. It was merely a smooth stone which this David took up, and yet it terrified a host of Goliaths.

When the fame of this book reached the South, the poor,

* This cannot be entirely accurate, since in the *Appeal*, Walker several times refers to his extensive travels through the South and what he calls the West—by which he probably meant States such as Alabama or Tennessee. He refers, also, specifically, to his having been present at a revival meeting in South Carolina. It is possible, but not likely, that these trips were made sometime after his original visit to Boston—the date of which is uncertain—and his establishing himself in the clothing business there in 1827.

** Martha Gruening, in her sketch of Walker in the *Dictionary of American Biography*, finds strange the omission of the maiden name of Walker's wife. No doubt she was herself a fugitive slave; hence the use of only a first name may have been considered a necessary security measure—even in 1848.

cowardly, pusillanimous tyrants grew pale behind their cotton bags, and armed themselves to the teeth. They set watches to look after their happy and contented slaves. The Governor of Georgia wrote to the Hon. Harrison Grey [sic] Otis, the Mayor of Boston, requesting him to suppress the Appeal. His Honor replied to the Southern Censor, that he had no power nor disposition to hinder Mr. Walker from pursuing a lawful course in the utterance of his thoughts.

A company of Georgia men then bound themselves by an oath, that they would eat as little as possible until they had killed the youthful author. They also offered a reward of a thousand dollars for his head, and ten times as much for the live Walker.

His consort, with the solicitude of an affectionate wife, with some friends, advised him to go to Canada, lest he should be abducted. Walker said that he had nothing to fear from such a pack of coward blood-hounds; but if he did go he would hurl back such thunder across the great lakes, that would cause them to tremble in their strong holds. Said he, "I will stand my ground. *Somebody must die in this cause.* I may be doomed to the stake and the fire, or to the scaffold tree, but it is not in me to falter if I can promote the work of emancipation."

He did not leave the country but was soon laid in the grave. It was the opinion of many that he was hurried out of life by the means of poison, but whether this was the case or not, the writer is not prepared to affirm.

He had many enemies, and not a few were his brethren whose cause he espoused. They said that he went too far, and was making trouble. So the Jews spoke of Moses. They valued the flesh-pots of Egypt more than the milk of Canaan. He died 1830 in Bridge street, at the hopeful and enthusiastic age of 34 years [sic]. His ruling passion blazed up in the hour of death, and threw an indescribable grandeur over the last dark scene. The heroic young man passed away without a struggle, and a few weeping friends

'Saw in death his eyelids close,
Calmly, as to a night's repose,
Like flowers at set of sun."

The personal appearance of Mr. Walker was prepossessing, being six feet in height, slender and well-proportioned. His hair was loose, and his complexion was dark.* His son, the only child he left, is now 18 years of age, and is said to resemble his father; he now resides at Charlestown, Mass., with his mother, Mrs. Dewson.

Mr. Walker was a faithful member of the Methodist Church at Boston, whose pastor is the venerable father Snowden.

The reader thus has a brief notice of the life and character of David Walker.

Thus closes Garnet's "Sketch."

---

* I know no other description of Walker's person; and no likeness of him is known to exist. Professor Leon F. Litwack lists Walker as a mulatto, but it would be interesting to know his source of information. All that is known for certain is that both his parents were Negroes—one, a slave—and that Mr. Garnet describes him in the above terms—having spoken with his widow. See, L. F. Litwack, *North of Slavery: The Negro in the Free States, 1790-1860* (Chicago, 1961, p. 182).

V: THE APPEAL'S IMMEDIATE IMPACT

As we have already noted, the decade of the 1820's was one of intense slave unrest. Beginning in 1829 and persisting through 1831 there prevailed simply extraordinary rebelliousness.* The slaveholding class was driven frantic. Central to this picture is Walker's *Appeal.*

Walker personally supervised the printing and the distribution of his work; apparently it was being distributed by October, 1829. How many copies he printed is not known but it must have been many hundreds and probably a few thousands—certainly before his death in 1830, a third edition was produced and was being circulated. He used the mails and he also succeeded in having copies of the pamphlet carried by individuals for distribution by them. Evidence indicates that such distribution was accomplished particularly by ship. Walker lived and worked near the sea; maritime employment was very common for free Negroes—indeed, there were not many merchant ships that did not have some Negro men among their crews prior to the Civil War. Moreover, it is certain that white men also served as distributors of this *Appeal,* and some of them lived in the South.

The *Appeal* reached the hands of free Negroes and of slaves in the South. Note of this fact was taken by Governor John Forsyth of Georgia, in a communication to the State Legislature, December 21, 1829, in which he referred to a recent conspiracy in Georgetown, South Carolina and "the late fires in Augusta and Savannah" set by slaves. It is germane to add that this same Governor, back in May, 1829 had sent to the U.S. Secretary of War, John Eaton, an urgent appeal for arms, "to protect the people of the state in case of slave revolt." At

* For details, see my *American Negro Slave Revolts,* pp. 281-292.

the same time—that is on May 6, 1829—the Governor had sent a note to Major-General W.T. Montgomery, in command of the State Militia at Augusta, to be on particular alert. It is worth adding that in August, 1829, the Governor of Virginia had information that alarmed him, and he sent additional arms into the counties of Gloucester, Isle of Wight and Mathews.

In his December, 1829 communication to the Legislature, Governor Forsyth specifically mentioned receiving a letter from the Mayor of Savannah, "informing me that sixty pamphlets of a highly seditious character had been seized by the police of the city." The description that followed identifies this as the work of Walker; the Governor added the information that the pamphlets had been "carried to Savannah by the Steward of some vessel (a white man), and delivered by him to a negro preacher for distribution."

The Mayor of Savannah also wrote to Mayor Otis of Boston informing him that his city was the source of a "highly inflammatory" work and begging that something be done to stop it. The Governor also wrote in a similar vein to Mayor Otis. Otis sent an official emissary to Walker's shop to get the facts; Walker told the man that the pamphlet was sent out by him, that he was its author and that he intended to keep on doing exactly what the Mayor of Savannah and the Governor of Georgia wanted him not to do. Mayor Otis did issue a warning to ships' captains sailing out of Boston to be on the look-out for seditious cargo; on the other hand, he replied to the Georgia Mayor and Governor that Walker had violated no Massachusetts law and that therefore—much as all sensible people regretted what he wrote and what he was doing—he could not be stopped legally.

In January, 1830, the Mayor of Richmond, Virginia, reported the finding of a copy of the same pamphlet in the home of a recently deceased free Negro; in the same year and same city another free Negro, Thomas Lewis, was found to possess thirty copies of the fearful thing.

A white printer in Milledgeville, Georgia, Elijah H. Burritt, was accused in February, 1830, of introducing this work within the State, and "was finally forced to flee for his life in the middle of the night when a hostile mob attacked his dwelling."* The Governor of Georgia wrote to Mayor Otis about Burritt, stating that a letter from Walker to Burritt had come into the possession of local authorities. According to the Georgia Governor, Walker's letter stated that he had mailed twenty copies of the *Appeal* to Burritt, in accordance with the latter's request; the Governor asked Otis to obtain a copy of the letter Burritt had written to Walker, so that he might be prosecuted successfully. Otis, however, refused to undertake this and so Burritt was driven from the State by violence.

Copies of the *Appeal* also were found early in 1830 in New Orleans. In May one James Smith of Boston (whether white or Negro is not known) was convicted of circulating the *Appeal* and sentenced to a year's imprisonment in that city.

The Reverend Samuel J. May, in his *Some Recollections of the Anti-Slavery Conflict* (Boston, 1869, p. 134), states that two missionaries to the Cherokee Indians in Georgia—Reverends Worcester and Butler—"were maltreated and imprisoned in 1829 or 1830, for having one of Walker's pamphlets, as well as for admitting some colored children into their Indian school."

The discovery of the pamphlet in Walker's home state—where slave disaffection was especially rife—created terrific

---

* The quoted words are those of Merle Curti, from his *The Learned Blacksmith, the Life and Journals of Elihu Burritt* (N. Y., 1937, p. 118n.) Elijah was the brother of this famous pacifist, publicist and linguist. Professor Curti does not mention, however, the Walker pamphlet although it is because of possessing copies that Elijah was forced to flee. That he safely reached the North appears from a letter S. S. Jocelyn wrote to W. L. Garrison, dated New Haven, July 12, 1832, asking that *The Liberator* be sent Burritt at Berlin, Conn.—"the gentleman who suffers so much on acct. of Walker's pamphlet. I had an interview with him yesterday—he is a noble soul—lived 20 years in Gao.—has facts on the subject of slavery most horrible." This is from the MS Letters to Garrison in the Boston Public Library, quoted in my *To Be Free* (N. Y., 1948, p. 202).

concern. Copies were reported from Fayetteville, Wilmington, Chapel Hill, Newbern and Hillsborough. In August, 1830, a free Negro in Walker's home city of Wilmington brought a copy to the police. A slave, unnamed, who had acted as distributor of the *Appeal,* was arrested, but refused—although no doubt highly persuasive methods were used—to implicate others or to tell how many he had spread about. Spies were used in Fayetteville in order to discover the source of the pamphlet there, but said a report to the Governor, dated September 3, 1830, "altho this plan has been sometime in operation, it has yet developed nothing that ought to excite our alarm."

Southern newspapers—as the *Richmond Enquirer* and the *Richmond Whig*—devoted editorials to "The Pamphlet" to quote the title in the former paper's comment. Secret sessions of the Legislatures of Georgia and of North Carolina were convened by the Governors in order to discuss how best to deal with the threat contained in the *Appeal* and its appearance in their States; there and elsewhere in the South much additional legislation of a repressive and precautionary nature was enacted, particularly from 1829 to the Spring of 1831. In 1829, Georgia forbade the teaching of reading and writing to slaves and to free Negroes; in 1830 North Carolina and Louisiana passed a similar prohibition applicable to slaves. Virginia, in April, 1831, prohibited the assembling of free Negroes for purposes of instruction in reading and writing. From 1829 to early 1831, Georgia, North Carolina and Mississippi passed laws providing heavy penalties for any individuals (death for Negroes) engaged in the dissemination of anti-slavery material. During the same period Georgia and North Carolina enacted quarantine laws for all ships carrying free Negroes, the period of quarantine to last for 30 to 40 days respectively.

Many precautionary acts of a miscellaneous character were passed during these months. Thus, North Carolina passed laws punishing any who aided runaway slaves, providing for measures to combat maroons,* forbidding the cohabitation of free Negroes and slaves (one result of which had been—David Walker!), and the marriage of free Negroes and whites. Louisiana required all Negroes freed since 1825 to leave, and North Carolina ordered all Negroes emancipated after 1830 to leave within ninety days.

There was another type of political activity relating to slavery in the South in the months of the appearance of the Walker torch. In a constitutional convention held, 1829-1830 in Virginia, there was some discussion—especially by delegates from the western section of the State—about the harmfulness of slavery. According to some Virginians, one of the factors producing the marked unrest that appeared among slaves in that State—as elsewhere—was the (mistaken) belief among some of them that the main purpose of that Convention was to reach agreement on the termination of slavery.

In Kentucky, during the same period, there was an unsuccessful effort to hold a constitutional convention; among those who sought such a convention, in 1829, there was the desire to at least consider how to mitigate, if not terminate, the evils of slavery. In 1830 a bill for the purpose of ending slavery actually was introduced into the Kentucky legislature, but its consideration was postponed, indefinitely, by a vote of 18 to 11.

Walker's *Appeal* certainly was the subject of much thought and discussion within the developing anti-slavery movement. As we have seen, in the case of Garnet, its influence was enduring; in addition, it made a notable impact at once. We have earlier noticed the repeated comments upon it coming

* These were outlying fugitive slaves who, in many instances and throughout the history of slavery, conducted a kind of guerrilla warfare against the plantations. In these days of renewed interest—if that is the correct word—about guerrilla warfare it is relevant to note that slaves had developed the art long before the Pentagon showed concern. On maroons in the United States, see my *To Be Free* (N. Y., 1948, pp. 11-30).

from Benjamin Lundy and William Lloyd Garrison in 1830 in their *Genius of Universal Emancipation*. In the earliest issues, in 1831, of Garrison's *Liberator*, there also appeared extended consideration of Walker's work and of his life—and of his sudden, early and still mysterious death on June 28, 1830.

Among the significant responses induced by Walker's work within Abolitionist circles was the exchange between a Negro of Philadelphia, who signed himself, "Leo," and Garrison. The letter from Philadelphia was dated January 21, 1831 and was published, with a reply from the Editor, in the issue of January 29, 1831. This exchange, in full, was as follows:

> Sir—I have received and read with great satisfaction the first two numbers of the Liberator, with the exception of the notice you have taken of Walker's Appeal, which production I have ever been opposed to (1)—opposed to, in the first place, not because he is a man of color, but because I do not believe that he wrote it; for the matter brought forward in said pamphlet is the result of more reading than could have fallen to the lot of that man, and, at the same time, left him so vulgar as he has been represented to me. (2)—Besides, sir, he could never have read all the authors quoted in this book, and seen of what true greatness consisted, and then bestowed such unbounded praise upon one whose name the political, the moral, and the religious world will be found equally indifferent about handing to those who may come after us. (3)—To say nothing of the excellent criticisms upon the speeches of the most talented men of the age—all of which discover to us a greater degree of education than we have any reason to believe that he possessed.
>
> I am aware, sir, that I differ very widely from many of those with whom I am intimately connected; for some of them are so infatuated as to believe it an inspired work. Such inspiration is passing strange to me.
>
> We are forbidden, by high authority, to do evil that good may come. Why then cast this firebrand so injudiciously among the stubble? Behold its injurious effects! In many

of the southern states, the free people of color enjoyed some privileges and good situations, which not only afforded them the means of support but also of education—so that the rusty mind was daily becoming bright, and its brilliancy beaming forth to the destruction of prejudice. These privileges are now taken away.

I am opposed to the pamphlet, therefore, in the second place, because I believe it to be at the bottom of the recent enactments of severe laws in the southern states, such as are too notorious to be mentioned.

There is no man among us, who is more sensible of his political degradation than I am; but, at the same time, I am unwilling to resort to any dishonorable means of deliverance—such as Walker points out.

To this, Garrison replied this way:

(1) We know not wherein we differ from 'Leo' in his view of the pamphlet. We have repeatedly expressed our disapprobation of its general spirit. It contains, however, many valuable truths and seasonable warnings.

(2) We are surprised at this incredulity. Mr. Walker was personally unknown to us; but we are assured by those who intimately knew him, that his Appeal was an exact transcript of his daily conversations; that, within the last four years, he was hurtfully indefatigable in his studies; that he was not 'vulgar,' either in manners or language; and that he was a blameless professor of religion. The historical facts which he has collected were too familiar to have required extraordinary research. Besides, the internal evidence of the pamphlet clearly substantiates its authorship.

(3) We cannot find that there is any other individual extolled than the venerable and worthy bishop Richard Allen*

---

* Richard Allen (1760-1831) was the founder and first Bishop of the African Methodist Episopal Church. Allen, born a slave in Philadelphia, lived for some years in Delaware. He was able to purchase his freedom; at the first general conference of the Methodist Church, in 1784, he was accepted as a Minister; he traveled and preached with bishop Asbury and from 1786 lived in Philadelphia, preaching occasionally. Jim Crow Christianity induced

of Philadelphia. Surely our correspondent cannot mean to deny *him* the tribute of merit which Mr. Walker bestowed?

Before turning to an examination of the *Appeal* itself, it is necessary to consider the mystery of Walker's death. Statements concerning this vary from those which positively affirm that his death was a natural one to those which assert that he was murdered.**

The verdict of "cause for suspicion, but no definite conclusion possible"—which is the position taken by Garnet, as we have seen—seems to be the soundest one given available evidence. In addition to the remarks of Garnet—and it is to be remembered that these were based upon an interview with Walker's widow—there is the following communication, published in *The Liberator,* January 22, 1831, under the headline, DEATH OF WALKER, and signed "A Colored Bostonian":

> Sir—Having been prompted, by the inquiries of the Journal & Tribune, to make some researches respecting the circumstances of the death of Walker, author of a flagitious pamphlet, so called; I have spared no pains to obtain correct information relative thereto. The result has not been satisfactory to me, and probably will not be to the public.

---

him to lead a movement that finally resulted in the creation of the AME Church. He was a leader in secular Negro organization also, and was actively anti-slavery. See Charles Wesley, *Richard Allen* (Washington, 1939) .

** Garrison's sons, in their biography, affirm that his death was natural; this is followed by Alice D. Adams and by R. A. Warner in his *New Haven Negroes* (New Haven, 1940, p. 100) ; J. S. Redding, on the other hand, declares that Walker himself went to Richmond to distribute his work, and there "was arrested and was never seen again." (*Op. cit.,* p. 91) This certainly is an error; it probably is based upon J. C. Carroll's statement that Walker was apprehended in 1830 in Richmond, while distributing his pamphlet. This also cannot be accurate, and probably results from a misreading of the archival sources in Richmond, which do refer to the presence of Walker's *Appeal* and *its* seizure, but not the seizure of its author.—J. C. Carroll, *Slave Insurrections in the United States* (Boston, 1938, p. 126).

The most I can learn is, that some one or other, recently from the south, spread a report in this city that a reward of $3,000 was offered by southern planters to any one who would take the life of Walker. The report is believed by many of our population, who have no higher source of intelligence, to be true. Many well-informed persons of color there are, however, who have a strong suspicion that Walker came to his end otherwise than by a usual visitation of the Providence of God. Whether their suspicion be groundless or not, is a question—a question, too, under circumstances hard to be answered. In cases of law, presumptive evidence, I believe, is valid. Why not in this case? Were I asked, what is the presumptive evidence? I should answer, Prejudice—Pride—Avarice—Bigotry—in a word, the self-love of a wicked country, which outweigh all civil, moral and religious principles contained therein. If murder and robbery, with their correspondent evils, are practiced by the refined part of society, ought it to be thought a wonder that a man, like Walker, should fall a victim to the vengeance of the public? Is it not well known by individuals, that the whole country has set the example for them for centuries, by imbruing their hands in innocent blood? Is it not the language of the country to every individual, 'Go and Do Likewise'?

Until other and more conclusive evidence appears—which is quite unlikely—the modern historian can only conclude that deep mystery surrounds the manner of David Walker's death in his 44th year. Neither doubt nor mystery, however, surrounds the indubitable fact that he immortalized himself with the production of his *Appeal to the Colored Citizens of the World*.

VI: THE APPEAL—YESTERDAY AND TODAY

Walker's *Appeal* is the first sustained written assault upon slavery and racism to come from a black man in the United States. This was the main source of its overwhelming power in its own time; this is the source of the great relevance and enormous impact that remain in it, deep as we are in the twentieth century.

Never before or since was there a more uncompromising and devastating attack upon the hypocrisy of a jim-crow Christianity. This was to be a basic theme in Garrisonian Abolitionism; it remains one of the powerful streams now agitating and forcing transformation in American life.

Never before or since was there a more passionate denunciation of the hypocrisy of the nation as a whole—democratic and fraternal and equalitarian and all the other words. And Walker does this not as one who hates the country but rather as one who hates the institutions which disfigure it and make it a hissing in the world. Walker makes explicit—quite remarkable for a work written in 1829—the Albatross that slavery and racism are to the United States diplomatically; today a commonplace, though a commonplace that has lost none of its force or truthfulness.

One of the basic themes of the Abolitionist movement was to be—especially in the 1830's and 1840's—opposition to the colonization movement. Walker's merciless attack upon this scheme the better to retain the slaves contains every argument subsequently put forward. Note is to be taken of Walker's insistence that the United States belongs to the black people at least as much as it does to the white—" . . . this country is as much ours as it is the whites," or again, "America is more our country than it is the whites—we have enriched it with our *blood* and *tears* . . .".

Part of the fury of Walker's attack upon colonizationism came because of his knowledge that while its main purpose was to help secure property in slaves, its inspiration was racism. We colored peoples, was his reply, will stay because this is our land; and we will stay and "their prejudice will be obliged to fall like lightning to the ground."

Walker is among the pioneer antagonists to racism. It is notable in this connection that he selects as his foe, one of the finest minds and personalities among the white population of the 18th and early 19th centuries—Thomas Jefferson. He selects him exactly because he is of the finest and because, as the author of the Declaration of Independence, as a slave-owner and as one who, in his *Notes on Virginia,** embraces—though with hesitation—the idea of the innate mental inferiority of Negro people, Jefferson symbolizes, as it were, the contradictions consuming the Republic.

Walker's specific argumentation need not be repeated, as the reader will see this for himself. It may be remarked that all of Walker's quotations from Jefferson—as all his other questions—are faithful to the original; the only change Walker makes is to italicize certain words in Jefferson's sentences. It will be worthwhile, however, to quote from the paragraph preceding the one with which Walker begins his citation, for this will explain the exceedingly tentative manner in which Jefferson did put forth his belief in inferiority—a rather advanced position for a white Virginian of the 18th century and alas a position markedly more advanced than that held by many white Americans one hundred and eighty years later!

* This was Jefferson's only full-length work, originally written in reply to questions put by the Secretary of the French Legation in Philadelphia. Jefferson revised his manuscript in 1782-83; it was first published, anonymously, in a small edition in Paris in 1784. Within the next five years, many other editions appeared in the United States and in England, France and Prussia.

Jefferson commences in this manner:

> The opinion that they are inferior in the faculties of reason and imagination, must be hazarded with extreme diffidence. To justify a general conclusion, requires many observations, even where the subject may be submitted to the anatomical knife, to optical glasses, to analysis by fire or by solvents. How much more then where it is a faculty, not a substance, we are examining; where it eludes the research of all the senses; where the conditions of its existence are various and variously combined; where the effects of those which are present or absent bid defiance to calculation; let me add, too, as a circumstance of great tenderness, where our conclusion would degrade a whole race of men from the rank in the scale of beings which their Creator may perhaps have given them. To our reproach it must be said, that though for a century and a half we have had under our eyes the races of black and of red men, they have never yet been viewed by us as subjects of natural history.

It is after this introduction that Jefferson goes on, as Walker quotes him, "I advance it, therefore, as a suspicion only . . ."; it is this to which Jefferson has reference when he writes, "therefore."

Walker's work conveys better than any other single book of which this writer has knowledge, the awful quality of *insult* and *indignity* that racism entails; the *outrageous* and *utterly cruel* character of this assault comes through in Walker's effort with great force.

It is a wholesomely sobering thought, too, that in two great historic questions of the nineteenth and the twentieth century —chattel slavery and racism—it is David Walker and not Thomas Jefferson who stands vindicated by the best thought of the present epoch.

Walker is unmerciful in attacking those who advocate acquiescence. Clearly here he is acting the part of the goad, the gadfly. Walker faces the problem facing all Negro authors writing within the white world—*i.e.*, the fact that the "enemy" is reading; he faces in this connection the particular problem of "washing dirty linen in public"—and before a hostile public. He resolves that problem by facing up to it and writing fiercely and without quarter.

While he is pitiless where he thinks faults and cowardice exist, his *Appeal* conveys at the same time a profound pride in his people and a deep awareness of their militancy and their discontent. In that sense, his words and his call—and his very being—are blasting replies to those of the past, and of the present, who find—or say they find—some special docility or passivity in Negro people, as contrasted with all other peoples of the world.

Walker's vision is large. He knows that if slavery persists, the Republic dies; he knows, too, that not only slavery but every vestige of discrimination and segregation must go; in that vein he attacks not only the slavery of the South, but the jim crow of the North.

His vision is vast, too, in his concept of a world community of colored peoples. This appears not only in the work's title, but explicitly and repeatedly in the text, as in his demand for the *"entire emancipation of your enslaved brethren all over the world"*—a thought italicized in the original. His demand also is unequivocal; he wants "the complete overthrow of the system of slavery in every part of the country." These qualities—worldwide scope and no equivocation—remind one of W.E.B. Du Bois. So, also, do Walker's passion and the sheer poetical force of much of his writing.

Walker emphasizes, also, as did Du Bois, the material and the economic motivations behind all the fine words and ingenious rationalization decorating the institution of slavery. He reminds one of Du Bois also in his almost worshipful attitude towards learning and education; in this, too, Walker is an important pioneer in the literature of the American Negro people. "I would crawl on my hands and knees through mud and mire, to the feet of a learned man. . .". One finds here not only the passion for truth per se, but also—again as in Du Bois—the awareness that mastering learning provided a powerful force to break the chains of slavery.

Walker makes clear that it is slaveowners, and racists, not white people, that he hates. He several times pays the warmest tribute to those among white people—and when he wrote they were not numerous—who had some idea of the abominable character of slavery and who acted in accordance with their knowledge. Of course, he makes crystal clear the existence of the hatred and feels it necessary—it still is necessary—to warn the racists not to be surprised that the hatred is there—"for if we are men, we cannot but hate you, while you are treating us like dogs."

Walker's main point is that slavery and racism are anti-human and that persistence in them will bring destruction. Hence both must go, and the oppressors must in time acknowledge the wrongs they have done. Walker's commitment is a final one; he several times states that he fully expects to be done to death for his views and his insistence upon expressing them publicly.

On the use of violence, Walker is somewhat ambiguous. He certainly is not enamored of it; rather, his position is about that of the Declaration of Independence; it repudiates both pacifism and terrorism. Walker, in fact, hopes for repentance on the part of the slaveowners and urges that with repentance they will gain redemption. He does make perfectly clear that it is not for them to feign horror at violence, for their institution was created through violence and its maintenance is a constant exercise in the use of violence.

Walker does urge resistance to violence and warns that should this begin it must be conducted with full seriousness, for most certainly the slaveowners have not been joking and will not act otherwise than without mercy and in deadly earnest. The religious theme that is so strong in Walker—and was so strong generally in pre-Civil War United States—comes out not only in his ideas of redemption and repentance, but also in his insistence that it is God's will one must implement. In connection with the manifestation of that Will he projects the possibility of a Messiah—an idea that appeared in Robert Alexander Young's pamphlet published a few months before his own, and one that very much was in Nat Turner's mind when he undertook his uprising some months later.

It is clear, then, that in Walker's *Appeal* one has a document of historic import. This is true not only because of the direct and considerable impact it had upon its own day. It is true also because it projects most of the arguments and questions that were to be used and raised in the next generation of decisive struggle against slavery.

It is of great historic moment, too, in that it brings forward repeated strands in Negro life and history: militancy, the need for unity within the United States, the vision of a world-wide unity of all colored peoples, the relationship between ending enslavement and a positive future for the United States, the unequivocal rejection of racism, the refusal to despair as to the future of the Republic, the demand for full equality, the passion for learning, and the knowledge that the acid test of the nation is the position therein of the Negro people. On the basis of the latter perception, Walker insists that it is the struggle against slavery that must take precedence over all other causes and efforts; therefore, he urges that "one continual cry would be raised in all parts of the confederacy and would cease only with the complete overthrow of the system of slavery, in every part of the country."

It is this that the Abolitionists as a whole soon comprehended; acting on that insight, they helped cleanse the country. When Walker wrote, in 1829, of the need for the "complete overthrow of the system of slavery" he certainly meant, as his work shows, the elimination of racism. His *Appeal*, being a work of genius, projected tasks for succeeding generations. This task—the destruction of jim crow—is a central one of the present generation of Americans. The nation could not survive with slavery in the nineteenth century; it will not survive with jim crow in the twentieth century.

* * *

The edition of Walker's *Appeal* reprinted in the pages that follow is the third and last, printed in 1830. It is printed exactly as in the original, with the exception that its paragraphing has been modernized. All spelling, punctuation, footnotes are as in the original. The reader will see occasionally the word, "Addition"; this is as given in the third edition of the work and Walker here is indicating to the reader that this is material not found in the first and/or second editions. In the original, also, Walker occasionally emphasized a point not only through punctuation or italics, etc.—all of which are herewith reproduced—but also by the placing of a representation of a pointing hand; this last has not been reproduced.

The titles of each of the three editions of the *Appeal* differed slightly; the reader has that of the third edition before him.* The title pages of the first two editions were as follows:

* Notice is to be taken of the fact that Walker used the term "citizens" in each of his three titles. Saunders Redding calls attention to this by italicizing the word "citizens" and remarking that this was a piece of "unconscious irony." Insofar as the Negro people—including those not slaves—were not considered citizens by the Federal government (a point made formal in the Dred Scott decision), the use of the word had an ironic flavor; whether or not it was "unconscious," is another matter. Walker certainly was aware that the rights of citizenship were denied the Negro people; hence his use of the term may well have been quite deliberate. Furthermore, such a title no doubt would be more distressing to the Governor of Georgia, for example, than one that carried the word "people" rather than "citizens." Also to be borne in mind is the fact that the word "citizen" still conveyed—when Walker was writing—revolutionary overtones from the days of the French Revolution; "citizen" in the late 18th and early 19th century carried something of the flavor of the word "comrade" in the late 19th and in the 20th centuries.

Walker, David. Appeal, in Four Articles, with a Preamble, to the Colored Citizens of the World, but in particular to Those of the U.S. Written in Boston, Mass. Sept. 28th, 1829. Boston, 1829.

Walker's Appeal, in Four Articles, together with a Preamble, to the Colored Citizens of the World, but in particular and very expressly to those of the United States of America. Written in Boston, in the State of Massachusetts, Sept. 28, 1829. Second Edition, With Corrections, &c. By David Walker. 1830.

The first edition came to 76 printed pages; the second to 80, and the third to 88. Libraries possessing one or more editions include the Boston Public Library, the Harvard University Library, the Cornell University Library, and the Schomburg Branch of the New York Public Library. The present reprinting is of the copy of the third edition in the latter Library.

In earlier pages, elucidation of references and biographical data concerning individuals found in the *Appeal* have been offered. There are, however, references to two additional works made by Walker that need annotation. One is to Butler's History of the United States. This has reference to the work by Frederick Butler (1766?-1843) : *A Complete History of the United States of America, embracing the whole period from the discovery of North America down to the year 1820* (Hartford, By the Author, 1821, 3 vols.) . The other is to Goldsmith's History of Greece. This refers to the history by the well-known Oliver Goldsmith, which appeared in several editions and printings. Probably, the one used by Walker was: Oliver Goldsmith, *The Grecian History, from the earliest state to the death of Alexander the Great* (Hartford, 1824, S. Andrus) . The same publisher put out a second edition of this work in 1826.

Here, then, is David Walker's *Appeal.*

61

Boston Decr 7th 1831

WALKER'S

APPEAL,

IN FOUR ARTICLES;

TOGETHER WITH

A PREAMBLE,

TO THE

COLOURED CITIZENS OF THE WORLD,

BUT IN PARTICULAR, AND VERY EXPRESSLY, TO THOSE OF

THE UNITED STATES OF AMERICA,

WRITTEN IN BOSTON, STATE OF MASSACHUSETTS,
SEPTEMBER 28, 1829.

═══════════

THIRD AND LAST EDITION,
WITH ADDITIONAL NOTES, CORRECTIONS, &c.

═══════════

Boston:
REVISED AND PUBLISHED BY DAVID WALKER.
. . . .
1830.

Original title page photographed.

It will be recollected, that I, in the first edition of my "Appeal,"* promised to demonstrate in the course of which, viz. in the course of my Appeal, to the satisfaction of the most incredulous mind, that we Coloured People of these United States, are, the most wretched, degraded and abject set of beings that ever lived since the world began, down to the present day, and, that, the white Christians of America, who hold us in slavery, (or, more properly speaking, pretenders to Christianity,) treat us more cruel and barbarous than any Heathen nation did any people whom it had subjected, or reduced to the same condition, that the Americans (who are, notwithstanding, looking for the Millennial day) have us. All I ask is, for a candid and careful perusal of this the third and last edition of my Appeal, where the world may see that we, the Blacks or Coloured People, are treated more cruel by the white Christians of America, than devils themselves ever treated a set of men, women and children on this earth.

It is expected that all coloured men, women and children,** of every nation, language and tongue under heaven, will try to procure a copy of this Appeal and read it, or get some one to read it to them, for it is designed more particularly for them. Let them remember, that though our cruel oppressors and murderers, may (if possible) treat us more cruel, as Pharoah did the children of Israel, yet the God of the Etheopeans, has been pleased to hear our moans in consequence of oppression; and the day of our redemption from abject wretchedness draweth near, when we shall be enabled, in the most extended sense of the word, to stretch forth our hands to the LORD Our GOD, but there must be a willingness on our part, for GOD to do these things for us, for we may be assured that he will not take us by the hairs of our head against our will and desire, and drag us from our very, mean, low and abject condition.

* See my Preamble in first edition, first page. See also 2nd edition, Article 1, page 9.

** Who are not deceitful, abject, and servile to resist the cruelties and murders inflicted upon us by the white slave holders, our enemies by nature.

APPEAL, &c.
PREAMBLE.

My dearly beloved Brethren and Fellow Citizens.

HAVING travelled over a considerable portion of these United States, and having, in the course of my travels, taken the most accurate observations of things as they exist—the result of my observations has warranted the full and unshaken conviction, that we, (coloured people of these United States,) are the most degraded, wretched, and abject set of beings that ever lived since the world began; and I pray God that none like us ever may live again until time shall be no more. They tell us of the Israelites in Egypt, the Helots in Sparta, and of the Roman Slaves, which last were made up from almost every nation under heaven, whose sufferings under those ancient and heathen nations, were, in comparison with ours, under this enlightened and Christian nation, no more than a cypher—or, in other words, those nations of antiquity, had but little more among them than the name and form of slavery; while wretchedness and endless miseries were reserved, apparently in a phial, to be poured out upon our fathers, ourselves and our children, by *Christian* Americans!

These positions I shall endeavour, by the help of the Lord, to demonstrate in the course of this APPEAL, to the satisfaction of the most incredulous mind—and may God Almighty, who is the Father of our Lord Jesus Christ, open your hearts to understand and believe the truth.

The *causes,* my brethren, which produce our wretchedness and miseries, are so very numerous and aggravating, that I believe the pen only of a Josephus or a Plutarch, can well

63

enumerate and explain them. Upon subjects, then, of such incomprehensible magnitude, so impenetrable, and so notorious, I shall be obliged to omit a large class of, and content myself with giving you an exposition of a few of those, which do indeed rage to such an alarming pitch, that they cannot but be a perpetual source of terror and dismay to every reflecting mind.

I am fully aware, in making this appeal to my much afflicted and suffering brethren, that I shall not only be assailed by those whose greatest earthly desires are, to keep us in abject ignorance and wretchedness, and who are of the firm conviction that Heaven has designed us and our children to be slaves and *beasts of burden* to them and their children. I say, I do not only expect to be held up to the public as an ignorant, impudent and restless disturber of the public peace, by such avaricious creatures, as well as a mover of insubordination—and perhaps put in prison or to death, for giving a superficial exposition of our miseries, and exposing tyrants. But I am persuaded, that many of my brethren, particularly those who are ignorantly in league with slave-holders or tyrants, who acquire their daily bread by the blood and sweat of their more ignorant brethren—and not a few of those too, who are too ignorant to see an inch beyond their noses, will rise up and call me cursed—Yea, the jealous ones among us will perhaps use more abject subtlety, by affirming that this work is not worth perusing, that we are well situated, and there is no use in trying to better our condition, for we cannot. I will ask one question here.—Can our condition be any worse?—Can it be more mean and abject? If there are any changes, will they not be for the better, though they may appear for the worst at first? Can they get us any lower? Where can they get us? They are afraid to treat us worse, for they know well, the day they do it they are gone. But against all accusations which may or can be preferred against me, I appeal to Heaven for my motive in writing—who knows that my object is, if possible, to awaken in the breasts of my afflicted, degraded and slumbering brethren, a spirit of inquiry and investigation respecting our miseries and wretchedness in this REPUBLICAN LAND OF LIBERTY!!!!!!

The sources from which our miseries are derived, and on which I shall comment, I shall not combine in one, but shall put them under distinct heads and expose them in their turn; in doing which, keeping truth on my side, and not departing from the strictest rules of morality, I shall endeavour to penetrate, search out, and lay them open for your inspection. If you cannot or will not profit by them, I shall have done *my* duty to you, my country and my God.

And as the inhuman system of *slavery*, is the *source* from which most of our miseries proceed, I shall begin with that *curse to nations,* which has spread terror and devastation through so many nations of antiquity, and which is raging to such a pitch at the present day in Spain and in Portugal. It had one tug in England, in France, and in the United States of America; yet the inhabitants thereof, do not learn wisdom, and erase it entirely from their dwellings and from all with whom they have to do. The fact is, the labour of slaves comes too cheap to the avaricious usurpers, and is (as they think) of such great utility to the country where it exists, that those who are actuated by sordid avarice only, overlook the evils, which will as sure as the Lord lives, follow after the good. In fact, they are so happy to keep in ignorance and degradation, and to receive the homage and the labour of the slaves, they forget that God rules in the armies of heaven and among the inhabitants of the earth, having his ears continually open to the cries, tears and groans of his oppressed people; and being a just and holy Being will at one day appear fully in behalf of the oppressed, and arrest the progress of the avaricious oppressors; for although the destruction of the oppressors God may not effect by the oppressed, yet the Lord our God will bring other destructions upon them—for not unfrequently will he cause them to rise up one against another, to be split and divided, and to oppress each other, and sometimes to open hostilities with sword in hand.

Some may ask, what is the matter with this united and happy people?—Some say it is the cause of political usurpers, tyrants, oppressors, &c. But has not the Lord an oppressed and suffering people among them? Does the Lord condescend to hear their cries and see their tears in consequence of oppression? Will he let the oppressors rest comfortably and happy always? Will he not cause the very children of the oppressors to rise up against them, and ofttimes put them to death? "God works in many ways his wonders to perform."

I will not here speak of the destructions which the Lord brought upon Egypt, in consequence of the oppression and consequent groans of the oppressed—of the hundreds and thousands of Egyptians whom God hurled into the Red Sea for afflicting his people in their land—of the Lord's suffering people in Sparta or Lacedemon, the land of the truly famous Lycurgus—nor have I time to comment upon the cause which produced the fierceness with which Sylla usurped the title, and absolutely acted as dictator of the Roman people—the conspiracy of Cataline—the conspiracy against, and murder of Caesar in the Senate house—the spirit with which Marc Antony made himself master of the commonwealth—his associating Octavius and Lipidus with himself in power— their dividing the provinces of Rome among themselves— their attack and defeat, on the plains of Phillippi, of the last defenders of their liberty, (Brutus and Cassius)—the tyranny of Tiberius, and from him to the final overthrow of Constantinople by the Turkish Sultan, Mahomed II. A.D. 1453.

I say, I shall not take up time to speak of the *causes* which produced so much wretchedness and massacre among those heathen nations, for I am aware that you know too well, that God is just, as well as merciful!—I shall call your attention a few moments to that *Christian* nation, the Spaniards—while I shall leave almost unnoticed, that avaricious and cruel people, the Portuguese, among whom all true hearted Christians and lovers of Jesus Christ, must evidently see the judgments of God displayed. To show the judgments of God upon the Spaniards, I shall occupy but a little time, leaving a plenty of room for the candid and unprejudiced to reflect.

All persons who are acquainted with history, and particularly the Bible, who are not blinded by the God of this world, and are not actuated solely by avarice—who are able to lay aside prejudice long enough to view candidly and impartially, things as they were, are, and probably will be— who are willing to admit that God made man to serve Him *alone,* and that man should have no other Lord or Lords but Himself—that God Almighty is the *sole proprietor* or *master* of the WHOLE human family, and will not on any consideration admit of a colleague, being unwilling to divide his glory with another—and who can dispense with prejudice long enough to admit that we are *men,* notwithstanding our *improminent noses* and *woolly heads,* and believe that we feel for our fathers, mothers, wives and children, as well as the whites do for theirs.—I say, all who are permitted to see and believe these things, can easily recognize the judgments of God among the Spaniards. Though others may lay the cause of the fierceness with which they cut each other's throats, to some other circumstances, yet they who believe that God is a God of justice, will believe that SLAVERY *is the principal cause.*

While the Spaniards are running about upon the field of battle cutting each other's throats, has not the Lord an afflicted and suffering people in the midst of them, whose cries and groans in consequence of oppression are continually pouring into the ears of the God of justice? Would they not cease to cut each other's throats, if they could? But how can they? The very support which they draw from government to aid them in perpetrating such enormities, does it not arise in a great degree from the wretched victims of oppression among them? And yet they are calling for PEACE!— PEACE!! Will any peace be given unto them? Their destruction may indeed be procrastinated awhile, but can it continue long, while they are oppressing the Lord's people? Has He not the hearts of all men in His hand? Will he suffer one part of his creatures to go on oppressing another like brutes always, with impunity? And yet, those avaricious wretches are calling for PEACE!!!! I declare, it does appear to me, as though some nations think God is asleep, or that he made the Africans for nothing else but to dig their mines and work their farms, or they cannot believe history, sacred or profane.

I ask every man who has a heart, and is blessed with the privilege of believing—Is not God a God of justice to *all* his creatures? Do you say he is? Then if he gives peace and tranquillity to tyrants, and permits them to keep our fathers, our mothers, ourselves and our children in eternal ignorance and wretchedness, to support them and their families, would he be to us a God of *justice?* I ask, O ye *Christians*!!! who hold us and our children in the most abject ignorance and degradation, that ever a people were afflicted with since the world began—I say, if God gives you peace and tranquillity, and suffers you thus to go on afflicting us, and our children, who have never given you the least provocation— would he be to us *a God of justice?* If you will allow that we are MEN, who feel for each other, does not the blood of our fathers and of us their children, cry aloud to the Lord of Sabaoth against you, for the cruelties and murders with which you have, and do continue to afflict us. But it is time for me to close my remarks on the suburbs, just to enter more fully into the interior of this system of cruelty and oppression.

ARTICLE I.

OUR WRETCHEDNESS IN
CONSEQUENCE OF SLAVERY.

MY BELOVED BRETHREN:—The Indians of North and of South America—the Greeks—the Irish, subjected under the king of Great Britain—the Jews, that ancient people of the Lord—the inhabitants of the islands of the sea—in fine, all the inhabitants of the earth, (except however, the sons of Africa) are called *men,* and of course are, and ought to be free. But we, (coloured people) and our children are *brutes!!* and of course are, and *ought to be* SLAVES to the American people and their children forever!! to dig their mines and work their farms; and thus go on enriching them, from one generation to another with our *blood* and our *tears!!!!*

I promised in a preceding page to demonstrate to the satisfaction of the most incredulous, that we, (coloured people of these United States of America) are the *most wretched, degraded* and *abject* set of beings that `ever lived` since the world began, and that the white Americans having reduced us to the wretched state of *slavery,* treat us in that condition *more cruel* (they being an enlighted and Christian people,) than any heathen nation did any people whom it had reduced to our condition. These affirmations are so well confirmed in the minds of all unprejudiced men, who have taken the trouble to read histories, that they need no elucidation from me. But to put them beyond all doubt, I refer you in the first place to the children of Jacob, or of Israel in Egypt, under Pharaoh and his people. Some of my brethren do not know who Pharaoh and the Egyptians were—I know it to be a fact, that some of them take the Egyptians to have been a gang of *devils,* not knowing any better, and that they

(Egyptians) having got possession of the Lord's people, treated them *nearly* as cruel as *Christian Americans* do us, at the present day. For the information of such, I would only mention that the Egyptians, were Africans or coloured people, such as we are—some of them yellow and others dark —a mixture of Ethiopians and the natives of Egypt—about the same as you see the coloured people of the United States at the present day.—I say, I call your attention then, to the children of Jacob, while I point out particularly to you his son Joseph, among the rest, in Egypt.

"And Pharaoh, said unto Joseph, thou shalt be over my house, and according unto thy word shall all my people be ruled: only in the throne will I be greater than thou."*

"And Pharaoh said unto Joseph, see, I have set thee over all the land of Egypt."**

"And Pharaoh said unto Joseph, I am Pharaoh, and without thee shall no man lift up his hand or foot in all the land of Egypt."***

Now I appeal to heaven and to earth, and particularly to the American people themselves, who cease not to declare that our condition is not *hard,* and that we are comparatively satisfied to rest in wretchedness and misery, under them and their children. Not, indeed, to show me a coloured President, a Governor, a Legislator, a Senator, a Mayor, or an Attorney at the Bar.—But to show me a man of colour, who holds the low office of a Constable, or one who sits in a Juror Box, even on a case of one of his wretched brethren, throughout this great Republic!!—But let us pass Joseph the son of Israel a little farther in review, as he existed with that heathen nation.

"And Pharaoh called Joseph's name Zaphnathpaaneah; and he gave him to wife Asenath the daughter of Potipherah priest of On. And Joseph went out over all the land of Egypt."*

* See Genesis, chap. xli. ** xli. 44. *** xli. 44.
* xli. 45.

Compare the above, with the American institutions. Do they not institute laws to prohibit us from marrying among the whites? I would wish, candidly, however, before the Lord, to be understood, that I would not give a *pinch of snuff* to be married to any white person I ever saw in all the days of my life. And I do say it, that the black man, or man of colour, who will leave his own colour (provided he can get one, who is good for any thing) and marry a white woman, to be a double slave to her, just because she is *white,* ought to be treated by her as he surely will be, viz: as a NIGER!!!! It is not, indeed, what I care about inter-marriages with the whites, which induced me to pass this subject in review; for the Lord knows, that there is a day coming when they will be glad enough to get into the company of the blacks, not-withstanding, we are, in this generation, levelled by them, almost on a level with the brute creation: and some of us they treat even worse than they do the brutes that perish. I only made this extract to show how much lower we are held, and how much more cruel we are treated by the Americans, than were the children of Jacob, by the Egyptians.— We will notice the sufferings of Israel some further, under *heathen Pharaoh,* compared with ours under the *enlightened Christians of America.*

"And Pharaoh spake unto Joseph, saying, thy father and thy brethren are come unto thee:"

"The land of Egypt is before thee: in the best of the land make thy father and brethren to dwell; in the land of Goshen let them dwell: and if thou knowest any men of activity among them, then make them rulers over my cattle."*

I ask those people who treat us so *well,* Oh! I ask them, where is the most barren spot of land which they have given unto us? Israel had the most fertile land in all Egypt. Need I mention the very notorious fact, that I have known a poor man of colour, who laboured night and day, to acquire a little money, and having acquired it, he vested it in a small piece of land, and got him a house erected thereon, and

* Genesis, chap. xlvii, 5, 6.

having paid for the whole, he moved his family into it, where he was suffered to remain but nine months, when he was cheated out of his property by a white man, and driven out of door! And is not this the case generally? Can a man of colour buy a piece of land and keep it peaceably? Will not some white man try to get it from him, even if it is in a *mud hole?* I need not comment any farther on a subject, which all, both black and white, will readily admit. But I must, really, observe that in this very city, when a man of colour dies, if he owned any real estate it most generally falls into the hands of some white person. The wife and children of the deceased may weep and lament if they please, but the estate will be kept snug enough by its white possessor.

But to prove farther that the condition of the Israelites was better under the Egyptians than ours is under the whites. I call upon the professing Christians, I call upon the philanthropist, I call upon the very tyrant himself, to show me a page of history, either sacred or profane, on which a verse can be found, which maintains, that the Egyptians heaped the *insupportable insult* upon the children of Israel, by telling them that they were not of the *human family*. Can the whites deny this charge? Have they not, after having reduced us to the deplorable condition of slaves under their feet, held us up as descending originally from the tribes of *Monkeys* or *Orang-Outangs?* O! my God! I appeal to every man of feeling—is not this insupportable? Is it not heaping the most gross insult upon our miseries, because they have got us under their feet and we cannot help ourselves? Oh! pity us we pray thee, Lord Jesus, Master.—Has Mr. Jefferson declared to the world, that we are inferior to the whites, both in the endowments of our bodies and of minds? It is indeed surprising, that a man of such great learning, combined with such excellent natural parts, should speak so of a set of men in chains. I do not know what to compare it to, unless, like putting one wild deer in an iron cage, where it will be secured, and hold another by the side of the same, then let it go, and expect the one in the cage to run as fast as the one at liberty. So far, my brethren, were the Egyptians from heaping these insults upon their slaves, that Pharoah's daughter took Moses, a son of Israel for her own, as will appear by the following.

"And Pharoah's daughter said unto her, [Moses' mother] take this child away, and nurse it for me, and I will pay thee thy wages. And the woman took the child [Moses] and nursed it.

"And the child grew, and she brought him unto Pharoah's daughter and he became her son. And she called his name Moses: and she said because I drew him out of the water."*

In all probability, Moses would have become Prince Regent to the throne, and no doubt, in process of time but he would have been seated on the throne of Egypt. But he had rather suffer shame, with the people of God, than to enjoy pleasures with that wicked people for a season. O! that the coloured people were long since of Moses' excellent disposition, instead of courting favour with, and telling news and lies to our *natural enemies,* against each other—aiding them to keep their hellish chains of slavery upon us. Would we not long before this time, have been respectable men, instead of such wretched victims of oppression as we are? Would they be able to drag our mothers, our fathers, our wives, our children and ourselves, around the world in chains and hand-cuffs as they do, to dig up gold and silver for them and theirs? This question, my brethren, I leave for you to digest; and may God Almighty force it home to your hearts. Remember that unless you are united, keeping your tongues within your teeth, you will be afraid to trust your secrets to each other, and thus perpetuate our miseries under the *Christians*!!!!! Addition.— Remember, also to lay humble at the feet of our Lord and Master Jesus Christ, with prayers and fastings. Let our enemies go on with their butcheries, and at once fill up their cup. Never make an attempt to gain our freedom or *natural right,* from under our cruel oppressors and murderers, until you see your way

* See Exodus, chap. ii. 9, 10.

clear*—when that hour arrives and you move, be not afraid or dismayed; for be you assured that Jesus Christ the King of heaven and of earth who is the God of justice and of armies, will surely go before you. And those enemies who have for hundreds of years stolen our *rights,* and kept us ignorant of Him and His divine worship, he will remove. Millions of whom, are this day, so ignorant and avaricious, that they cannot conceive how God can have an attribute of justice, and show mercy to us because it pleased Him to make us black—which colour, Mr. Jefferson calls unfortunate!!!!!! As though we are not as thankful to our God, for having made us as it pleased himself, as they (the whites,) are for having made them white. They think because they hold us in their infernal chains of slavery, that we wish to be white, or of their color—but they are dreadfully deceived —we wish to be just as it pleased our Creator to have made us, and no avaricious and unmerciful wretches, have any business to make slaves of, or hold us in slavery. How would they like for us to make slaves of, and hold them in cruel slavery, and murder them as they do us?—But is Mr. Jefferson's assertions true? viz. "that it is unfortunate for us that our Creator has been pleased to make us *black.*" We will not take his say so, for the fact. The world will have an opportunity to see whether it is unfortunate for us, that our Creator *has made us* darker than the *whites.*

Fear not the number and education of our *enemies,* against whom we shall have to contend for our lawful right;

* It is not to be understood here, that I mean for us to wait until God shall take us by the hair of our heads and drag us out of abject wretchedness and slavery, nor do I mean to convey the idea for us to wait until our enemies shall make preparations, and call us to seize those preparations, take it away from them, and put every thing before us to death, in order to gain our freedom which God has given us. For you must remember that we are men as well as they. God has been pleased to give us two eyes, two hands, two feet, and some sense in our heads as well as they. They have no more right to hold us in slavery than we have to hold them, we have just as much right, in the sight of God, to hold them and their children in slavery and wretchedness, as they have to hold us, and no more.

guaranteed to us by our Maker; for why should we be afraid, when God is, and will continue, (if we continue humble) to be on our side?

The man who would not fight under our Lord and Master Jesus Christ, in the glorious and heavenly cause of freedom and of God—to be delivered from the most wretched, abject and servile slavery, that ever a people was afflicted with since the foundation of the world, to the present day—ought to be kept with all of his children or family, in slavery, or in chains, to be butchered by his *cruel enemies.*

I saw a paragraph, a few years since, in a South Carolina paper, which, speaking of the barbarity of the Turks, it said: "The Turks are the most barbarous people in the world— they treat the Greeks more like *brutes* than human beings." And in the same paper was an advertisement, which said: "Eight well built Virginia and Maryland *Negro fellows* and four *wenches* will positively be *sold* this day, *to the highest bidder!*" And what astonished me still more was, to see in this same *humane* paper!! the cuts of three men, with clubs and budgets on their backs, and an advertisment offering a considerable sum of money for their apprehension and de- livery. I declare, it is really so amusing to hear the Southern- ers and Westerners of this country talk about *barbarity,* that it is positively, enough to make a man *smile.*

The sufferings of the Helots among the Spartans, were somewhat severe, it is true, but to say that theirs, were as severe as ours among the Americans, I do most strenuously deny—for instance, can any man show me an article on a page of ancient history which specifies, that, the Spartans chained, and hand-cuffed the Helots, and dragged them from their wives and children, children from their parents, mothers from their suckling babes, wives from their husbands, driv- ing them from one end of the country to the other? Notice the Spartans were heathens, who lived long before our Divine Master made his appearance in the flesh.

Can Christian Americans deny these barbarous cruelties? Have you not, Americans, having subjected us under you, added to these miseries, by insulting us in telling us to our face, because we are helpless, that we are not of the human family? I ask you, O! Americans, I ask you, in the name of the Lord, can you deny these charges? Some perhaps may deny, by saying, that they never thought or said that we were not men. But do not actions speak louder than *words?*— have they not made provisions for the Greeks, and Irish? Nations who have never done the least thing for them, while *we,* who have enriched their country with our blood and tears—have dug up gold and silver for them and their children, from generation to generation, and are in more miseries than any other people under heaven, are not seen, but by comparatively, a handful of the American people? There are indeed, more ways to kill a dog, besides choking it to death with butter. Further—The Spartans or Lacedemonians, had some frivolous pretext, for enslaving the Helots, for they (Helots) while being free inhabitants of Sparta, stirred up an intestine commotion, and were, by the Spartans subdued, and made prisoners of war. Consequently they and their children were condemned to perpetual slavery.*

I have been for years troubling the pages of historians, to find out what our fathers have done to the *white Christians of America,* to merit such condign punishment as they have inflicted on them, and do continue to inflict on us their children. But I must aver, that my researches have hitherto been to no effect. I have therefore, come to the immoveable conclusion, that they (Americans) have, and do continue to punish us for nothing else, but for enriching them and their country. For I cannot conceive of any thing else. Nor will I ever believe otherwise, until the Lord shall convince me.

The world knows, that slavery as it existed among the Romans, (which was the primary cause of their destruction) was, comparatively speaking, no more than a *cypher,* when

---

* See Dr. Goldsmith's History of Greece—page 9. See also, Plutarch's Lives. The Helots subdued by Agis, king of *Sparta.*

compared with ours under the Americans. Indeed I should not have noticed the Roman slaves, had not the very learned and penetrating Mr. Jefferson said, "when a master was murdered, all his slaves in the same house, or within hearing, were condemned to death."*—Here let me ask Mr. Jefferson, (but he is gone to answer at the bar of God, for the deeds done in his body while living,) I therefore ask the whole American people, had I not rather die, or be put to death, than to be a slave to any tyrant, who takes not only my own, but my wife and children's lives by the inches? Yea, would I meet death with avidity far! far!! in preference to such *servile submission* to the murderous hands of tyrants. Mr. Jefferson's very severe remarks on us have been so extensively argued upon by men whose attainments in literature, I shall never be able to reach, that I would not have meddled with it, were it not to solicit each of my brethren, who has the spirit of a man, to buy a copy of Mr. Jefferson's "Notes on Virginia," and put it in the hand of his son. For let no one of us suppose that the refutations which have been written by our white friends are enough—they are *whites*—we are *blacks.*

We, and the world wish to see the charges of Mr. Jefferson refuted by the blacks *themselves,* according to their chance; for we must remember that what the whites have written respecting this subject, is other men's labours, and did not emanate from the blacks. I know well, that there are some talents and learning among the coloured people of this country, which we have not a chance to develop, in consequence of oppression; but our oppression ought not to hinder us from acquiring all we can. For we will have a chance to develop them by and by. God will not suffer us, always to be oppressed. Our sufferings will come to an *end,* in spite of all the Americans this side of *eternity.* Then we will want all the learning and talents among ourselves, and

* See his Notes on Virginia, page 210.

perhaps more, to govern ourselves.—"Every dog must have its day," the American's is coming to an end.

But let us review Mr. Jefferson's remarks respecting us some further. Comparing our miserable fathers, with the learned philosophers of Greece, he says: "Yet notwithstanding these and other discouraging circumstances among the Romans, their slaves were often their rarest artists. They excelled too, in science, insomuch as to be usually employed as tutors to their master's children; Epictetus, Terence and Phaedrus, were slaves,—but they were of the race of whites. It is not their *condition* then, but *nature,* which has produced the distinction."* See this, my brethren!! Do you believe that this assertion is swallowed by millions of the whites? Do you know that Mr. Jefferson was one of as great characters as ever lived among the whites? See his writings for the world, and public labours for the United States of America. Do you believe that the assertions of such a man, will pass away into oblivion unobserved by this people and the world? If you do you are much mistaken—See how the American people treat us—have we souls in our bodies? Are we men who have any spirits at all? I know that there are many *swell-bellied* fellows among us, whose greatest object is to fill their stomachs. Such I do not mean—I am after those who know and feel, that we are MEN, as well as other people; to them, I say, that unless we try to refute Mr. Jefferson's arguments respecting us, we will only establish them.

But the slaves among the Romans. Every body who has read history, knows, that as soon as a slave among the Romans obtained his freedom, he could rise to the greatest eminence in the State, and there was no law instituted to hinder a slave from buying his freedom. Have not the Americans instituted laws to hinder us from obtaining our freedom? Do any deny this charge? Read the laws of Virginia, North

* See his Notes on Virginia, page 211.

Carolina, &c. Further: have not the Americans instituted laws to prohibit a man of colour from obtaining and holding any office whatever, under the government of the United States of America? Now, Mr. Jefferson tells us, that our condition is not so hard, as the slaves were under the Romans!!!!!!

It is time for me to bring this article to a close. But before I close it, I must observe to my brethren that at the close of the first Revolution in this country, with Great Britain, there were but thirteen States in the Union, now there are twenty-four, most of which are slave-holding States, and the whites are dragging us around in chains and in handcuffs, to their new States and Territories to work their mines and farms, to enrich them and their children—and millions of them believing firmly that we being a little darker than they, were made by our Creator to be an inheritance to them and their children for even—the same as a parcel of *brutes*.

Are we MEN!!—I ask you, O my brethren! are we *MEN?* Did our Creator make us to be slaves to dust and ashes like ourselves? Are they not dying worms as well as we? Have they not to make their appearance before the tribunal of Heaven, to answer for the deeds done in the body, as well as we? Have we any other Master but Jesus Christ alone? Is he not their Master as well as ours?—What right then, have we to obey and call any other Master, but Himself? How we could be so *submissive* to a gang of men, whom we cannot tell whether they are *as good* as ourselves or not, I never could conceive. However, this is shut up with the Lord, and we cannot precisely tell—but I declare, we judge men by their works.

The whites have always been an unjust, jealous, unmerciful, avaricious and blood-thirsty set of beings, always seeking after power and authority.—We view them all over the confederacy of Greece, where they were first known to be any thing, (in consequence of education) we see them there, cutting each other's throats—trying to subject each other to wretchedness and misery—to effect which, they used all kinds of deceitful, unfair, and unmerciful means. We view them next in Rome, where the spirit of tyranny and deceit raged still higher. We view them in Gaul, Spain, and in Britain.—In fine, we view them all over Europe, together with what were scattered about in Asia and Africa, as heathens, and we see them acting more like devils than accountable men. But some may ask, did not the blacks of Africa, and the mulattoes of Asia, go on in the same way as did the whites of Europe. I answer, no—they never were half so avaricious, deceitful and unmerciful as the whites, according to their knowledge.

But we will leave the whites or Europeans as heathens, and take a view of them as Christians, in which capacity we see them as cruel, if not more so than ever. In fact, take them as a body, they are ten times more cruel, avaricious and unmerciful than ever they were; for while they were heathens, they were bad enough it is true, but it is positively a fact that they were not quite so audacious as to go and take vessel loads of men, women and children, and in cold blood, and through devilishness, throw them into the sea, and murder them in all kind of ways. While they were heathens, they were too ignorant for such barbarity. But being Christians, enlightened and sensible, they are completely prepared for such hellish cruelties.

Now suppose God were to give them more sense, what would they do? If it were possible, would they not *dethrone* Jehovah and seat themselves upon his throne? I therefore, in the name and fear of the Lord God of Heaven and of earth, divested of prejudice either on the side of my colour or that of the whites, advance my suspicion of them, whether they are *as good by nature* as we are or not. Their actions, since they were known as a people, have been the reverse, I do indeed suspect them, but this, as I before observed, is shut up with the Lord, we cannot exactly tell, it will be proved in succeeding generations.—The whites have had the essence of the gospel as it was preached by my master and his apostles—the Ethiopians have not, who are to have it in its meridian splendor—the Lord will give it to them to their satisfaction. I hope and pray my God, that they will make good use of it, that it may be well with them.*

---

* It is my solemn belief, that if ever the world becomes Christianized, (which must certainly take place before long) it will be through the means, under God of the *Blacks,* who are now held in wretchedness, and degradation, by the white *Christians* of the world, who before they learn to do justice to us before our Maker—and be reconciled to us, and reconcile us to them, and by that means have clear consciencies before God and man.— Send out Missionaries to convert the Heathens, many of whom after they cease to worship gods, which neither see nor hear, become ten times more the children of Hell, then ever they were, why what is the reason? Why the reason is obvious, they must learn to do justice at home, before they go into distant lands, to display their charity, Christianity, and benevolence; when they learn to do justice, God will accept their offering, (no man may think that I am against Missionaries for I am not, my object is to see justice done at home, before we go to convert the heathens.)

ARTICLE II.

OUR WRETCHEDNESS IN CONSEQUENCE OF IGNORANCE.

IGNORANCE, my brethren, is a mist, low down into the very dark and almost impenetrable abyss in which, our fathers for many centuries have been plunged. The Christians, and enlightened of Europe, and some of Asia, seeing the ignorance and consequent degradation of our fathers, instead of trying to enlighten them, by teaching them that religion and light with which God had blessed them, they have plunged them into wretchedness ten thousand times more intolerable, than if they had left them entirely to the Lord, and to add to their miseries, deep down into which they have plunged them tell them, that they are an *inferior* and *distinct race* of beings, which they will be glad enough to recall and swallow by and by. Fortune and misfortune, two inseparable companions, lay rolled up in the wheel of events, which have from the creation of the world, and will continue to take place among men until God shall dash worlds together.

When we take a retrospective view of the arts and sciences —the wise legislators—the Pyramids, and other magnificent buildings—the turning of the channel of the river Nile, by the sons of Africa or of Ham, among whom learning originated, and was carried thence into Greece, where it was improved upon and refined. Thence among the Romans, and all over the then enlightened parts of the world, and it has been enlightening the dark and benighted minds of men from then, down to this day. I say, when I view retrospectively, the renown of that once mighty people, the children of our great progenitor I am indeed cheered. Yea further, when I view that mighty son of Africa, HANNIBAL, one of the greatest generals of antiquity, who defeated and cut off so many thousands of the white Romans or murderers, and who carried his victorious arms, to the very gate of Rome, and I give it as my candid opinion, that had Carthage been well united and had given him good support, he would have carried that cruel and barbarous city by storm. But they were dis-united, as the coloured people are now, in the United States of America, the reason our natural enemies are enabled to keep their feet on our throats.

Beloved brethren—here let me tell you, and believe it, that the Lord our God, as true as he sits on his throne in heaven, and as true as our Saviour died to redeem the world, will give you a Hannibal, and when the Lord shall have raised him up, and given him to you for your possession, O my suffering brethren! remember the divisions and consequent sufferings of *Carthage* and of *Hayti*. Read the history particularly of Hayti, and see how they were butchered by the whites, and do you take warning. The person whom God shall give you, give him your support and let him go his length, and behold in him the salvation of your God. God will indeed, deliver you through him from your deplorable and wretched condition under the Christians of America. I charge you this day before my God to lay no obstacle in his way, but let him go.

The whites want slaves, and want us for their slaves, but some of them will curse the day they ever saw us. As true as the sun ever shone in its meridian splendor, my colour will root some of them out of the very face of the earth. They shall have enough of making slaves of, and butchering, and murdering us in the manner which they have. No doubt some may say that I write with a bad spirit, and that I being a black, wish these things to occur. Whether I write with a bad or a good spirit, I say if these things do not occur in their proper time, it is because of the world in which we live does not exist, and we are deceived with regard to its existence.—It is immaterial however to me, who believe,

83

or who refuse—though I should like to see the whites repent peradventure God may have mercy on them, some however, have gone so far that their cup must be filled.

But what need have I to refer to antiquity, when Hayti, the glory of the blacks and terror of tyrants, is enough to convince the most avaricious and stupid of wretches—which is at this time, and I am sorry to say it, plagued with that scourge of nations, the Catholic religion; but I hope and pray God that she may yet rid herself of it, and adopt in its stead the Protestant faith; also, I hope that she may keep peace within her borders and be united, keeping a strict look out for tyrants, for if they get the least chance to injure her, they will avail themselves of it, as true as the Lord lives in heaven. But one thing which gives me joy is, that they are men who would be cut off to a man, before they would yield to the combined forces of the whole world—in fact, if the whole world was combined against them, it could not do any thing with them, unless the Lord delivers them up.

Ignorance and treachery one against the other—a grovelling servile and abject submission to the lash of tyrants, we see plainly, my brethren, are not the natural elements of the blacks, as the Americans try to make us believe; but these are misfortunes which God has suffered our fathers to be enveloped in for many ages, no doubt in consequence of their disobedience to their maker, and which do, indeed, reign at this time among us, almost to the destruction of all other principles: for I must truly say, that ignorance, the mother of treachery and deceit, gnaws into our very vitals. Ignorance, as it now exists among us, produces a state of things, Oh my Lord! too horrible to present to the world. Any man who is curious to see the full force of ignorance developed among the coloured people of the United States of America, has only to go into the southern and western states of this confederacy, where, if he is not a tyrant, but has the feelings of a human being, who can feel for a fellow creature, he may see enough to make his very heart bleed! He may see there, a son take his mother, who bore almost the pains of death to give him birth, and by the command of a tyrant, strip her as naked as she came into the world, and apply the cow-hide to her, until she falls a victim to death in the road! He may see a husband take his dear wife, not unfrequently in a pregnant state, and perhaps far advanced, and beat her for an unmerciful wretch, until his infant falls a lifeless lump at her feet!

Can the Americans escape God Almighty? If they do, can he be to us a God of Justice? God is just, and I know it—for he has convinced me to my satisfaction—I cannot doubt him. My observer may see fathers beating their sons, mothers their daughters, and children their parents, all to pacify the passions of unrelenting tyrants. He may also, see them telling news and lies, making mischief one upon another. These are some of the productions of ignorance, which he will see practised among my dear brethren, who are held in unjust slavery and wretchedness, by avaricious and unmerciful tyrants, to whom, and their hellish deeds, I would suffer my life to be taken before I would submit. And when my curious observer comes to take notice of those who are said to be free, (which assertion I deny) and who are making some frivolous pretentions to common sense, he will see that branch of ignorance among the slaves assuming a more cunning and deceitful course of procedure.—He may see some of my brethren in league with tyrants, selling their own brethren into *hell upon earth,* not dissimilar to the exhibitions in Africa, but in a more secret, servile and abject manner. Oh Heaven! I am full!!! I can hardly move my pen!!! and as I expect some will try to put me to death, to strike terror into others, and to obliterate from their minds the notion of freedom, so as to keep my brethren the more secure in wretchedness, where they will be permitted to stay but a short time (whether tyrants believe it or not)—I shall give the world a development of facts, which are already witnessed in the courts of heaven. My observer may see some of those ignorant and treacherous creatures (coloured people) sneaking about in the large cities, endeavouring to find out all strange coloured people, where they work and where they reside, asking them questions, and trying to ascertain whether they are runaways or not, telling them, at the same time, that they always have been, are, and always will be, friends to their brethren; and, perhaps, that they themselves are absconders, and a thousand such treacherous lies to get the better information of the more ignorant!!! There have been and are at this day in Boston, New-York, Philadelphia, and Baltimore, coloured men, who are in league with tyrants, and who receive a great portion of their daily bread, of the moneys which they acquire from the blood and tears of their more miserable brethren, whom they scandalously delivered into the hands of our *natural enemies!!!!!!*

To show the force of degraded ignorance and deceit among us some farther, I will give here an extract from a paragraph, which may be found in the Columbian Centinel of this city, for September 9, 1829, on the first page of which, the curious may find an article, headed

"AFFRAY AND MURDER."

"Portsmouth, (Ohio) Aug. 22, 1829

A most shocking outrage was committed in Kentucky, about eight miles from this place, on 14th inst. A negro driver, by the name of Gordon, who had purchased in Maryland about sixty negroes, was taking them, assisted by an associate named Allen, and the wagoner who conveyed the baggage, to the Mississippi. The men were handcuffed and chained together, in the usual manner for driving those poor wretches, while the women and children were suffered to proceed without incumbrance. It appears that, by means of a file the negroes, unobserved, had succeeded in separating the iron which bound their hands, in such a way as to be able to throw them off at any moment. About 8 o'clock in the morning, while proceeding on the state road leading from Greenup to Vanceburg, two of them dropped their shackles and commenced a fight, when the wagoner

(Petit) rushed in with his whip to compel them to desist. At this moment, every negro was found to be perfectly at liberty; and one of them seizing a club, gave Petit a violent blow on the head, and laid him dead at his feet; and Allen, who came to his assistance, met a similar fate, from the contents of a pistol fired by another of the gang. Gordon was then attacked, seized and held by one of the negroes, whilst another fired twice at him with a pistol, the ball of which each time grazed his head, but not proving effectual, he was beaten with clubs, and left for dead. They then commenced pillaging the wagon, and with an axe split open the trunk of Gordon, and rifled it of the money, about $2,400. Sixteen of the negroes then took to the woods; Gordon, in the mean time, not being materially injured, was enabled, by the assistance of one of the women, to mount his horse and flee; pursued, however, by one of the gang on another horse, with a drawn pistol; fortunately he escaped with his life barely, arriving at a plantation, as the negro came in sight; who then turned about and retreated.

The neighbourhood was immediately rallied, and a hot pursuit given—which, we understand, has resulted in the capture of the whole gang and the recovery of the greatest part of the money. Seven of the negro men and one woman, it is said were engaged in the murders, and will be brought to trial at the next court in Greenupsburg.

Here, my brethren, I want you to notice particularly in the above article, the *ignorant* and *deceitful actions* of this coloured woman. I beg you to view it candidly, as for ETERNITY!!!! Here a *notorious wretch*, with two other confederates had SIXTY of them in a gang, driving them like *brutes*—the men all in chains and hand-cuffs, and by the help of God they got their chains and hand-cuffs thrown off, and caught two of the wretches and put them to death, and beat the other until they thought he was dead, and left him for dead; however, he deceived them, and rising from the ground, this *servile woman* helped him upon his horse, and he made his escape.

Brethren, what do you think of this? Was it the natural

fine feelings of this woman, to save such a wretch alive? I know that the blacks, take them half enlightened and ignorant, are more humane and merciful than the most enlightened and refined European that can be found in all the earth. Let no one say that I assert this because I am prejudiced on the side of my colour, and against the whites or Europeans. For what I write, I do it candidly, for my God and the good of both parties: Natural observations have taught me these things; there is a solemn awe in the hearts of the blacks, as it respects *murdering* men:* whereas the whites, (though they are great cowards) where they have the advantage, or think that there are any prospects of getting it, they murder all before them, in order to subject men to wretchedness and degradation under them. This is the natural result of pride and avarice. But I declare, the actions of this black woman are really insupportable. For my own part, I cannot think it was any thing but servile deceit, combined with the most gross ignorance: for we must remember that *humanity, kindness* and the *fear of the Lord,* does not consist in protecting *devils.*

Here is a set of wretches, who had *SIXTY* of them in a gang, driving them around the country like *brutes,* to dig up gold and silver for them, (which they will get enough of yet.) Should the lives of such creatures be spared? Are God and Mammon in league? What has the Lord to do with a gang of desperate wretches, who go *sneaking about the country like robbers*—light upon his people wherever they can get a chance, binding them with chains and hand-cuffs, beat and murder them as they would *rattle-snakes?* Are they not the Lord's enemies? Ought they not to be destroyed? Any person who will save such wretches from destruction, is fighting against the Lord, and will receive his just recompense. The black men acted like *blockheads.* Why did they not make sure of the wretch? He would have made sure of them, if he could. It is just the way with black men—eight

---

* Which is the reason the whites take the advantage of us.

88

white men can frighten fifty of them; whereas, if you can only get courage into the blacks, I do declare it, that one good black man can put to death six white men; and I give it as a fact, let twelve black men get well armed for battle, and they will kill and put to flight fifty whites.—The reason is, the blacks, once you get them started, they glory in death. The whites have had us under them for more than three centuries, murdering, and treating us like brutes; and, as Mr. Jefferson wisely said, they have never *found us out*—they do not know, indeed, that there is an unconquerable disposition in the breasts of the blacks, which, when it is fully awakened and put in motion, will be subdued, only with the destruction of the animal existence. Get the blacks started, and if you do not have a gang of tigers and lions to deal with, I am a deceiver of the blacks and of the whites.

How sixty of them could let that wretch escape unkilled, I cannot conceive—they will have to suffer as much for the two whom, they secured, as if they had put one hundred to death: If you commence, make sure work—do not trifle, for they will not trifle with you—they want us for their slaves, and think nothing of murdering us in order to subject us to that wretched condition—therefore, if there is an *attempt* made by us, kill or be killed. Now, I ask you, had you not rather be killed than to be a slave to a tyrant, who takes the life of your mother, wife, and dear little children? Look upon your mother, wife and children, and answer God Almighty! and believe this, that it is no more harm for you to kill a man, who is trying to kill you, than it is for you to take a drink of water when thirsty; in fact, the man who will stand still and let another murder him, is worse than an infidel, and, if he has common sense, ought not to be pitied.

The actions of this deceitful and ignorant coloured woman, in saving the life of a desperate wretch, whose avaricious and cruel object was to drive her, and her companions in miseries, through the country like cattle, to make his fortune on their carcasses, are but too much like that of thousands of our brethren in these states: if any thing is whispered by one, which has any allusion to the melioration of their dreadful condition, they run and tell tyrants, that they may be enabled to keep them the longer in wretchedness and miseries. Oh! coloured people of these United States, I ask you, in the name of that God who made us, have we, in consequence of oppression, nearly lost the spirit of man, and, in no very trifling degree, adopted that of brutes? Do you answer, no?—I ask you, then, what set of men can you point me to, in all the world, who are so abjectly employed by their oppressors, as we are by our *natural enemies?*

How can, Oh! how can those enemies but say that we and our children are not of the HUMAN FAMILY, but were made by our Creator to be an inheritance to them and theirs for ever? How can the slave-holders but say that they can bribe the best coloured person in the country, to sell his brethren for a trifling sum of money, and take that atrocity to confirm them in their avaricious opinion, that we were made to be slaves to them and their children? How could Mr. Jefferson but say,* "I advance it therefore as a suspicion only, that the blacks, whether originally a distinct race, or made distinct by time and circumstances, are *inferior* to the whites in the endowments both of body and mind?" "It," says he, "is not against experience to suppose, that different species of the same genus, or varieties of the same species, may possess different qualifications." [Here, my brethren, listen to him.] "Will not a lover of natural history, then, one who views the gradations in all the races of *animals* with the eye of philosophy, excuse an effort to keep those in the department of MAN as *distinct* as nature has formed them?" —I hope you will try to find out the meaning of this verse— its widest sense and all its bearings: whether you do or not, remember the whites do. This very verse, brethren, having emanated from Mr. Jefferson, a much greater philosopher the world never afforded, has in truth injured us more, and has been as great a barrier to our emancipation as any thing

* See his Notes on Virginia, page 213.

that has ever been advanced against us. I hope you will not let it pass unnoticed. He goes on further, and says: "This *unfortunate* difference of colour, and *perhaps of faculty*, is a powerful obstacle to the emancipation of these people. Many of their advocates, while they wish to vindicate the liberty of human nature are anxious also to preserve its *dignity* and *beauty*. Some of these, embarrassed by the question, 'What further is to be done with them?' join themselves in opposition with those who are actuated by sordid avarice only."

Now I ask you candidly, my suffering brethren in time, who are candidates for the eternal worlds, how could Mr. Jefferson but have given the world these remarks respecting us, when we are so submissive to them, and so much servile deceit prevail among ourselves—when we so *meanly* submit to their murderous lashes, to which neither the Indians nor any other people under Heaven would submit? No, they would die to a man, before they would suffer such things from men who are no better than themselves, and *perhaps not so good.* Yes, how can our friends but be embarrassed, as Mr. Jefferson says, by the question, "What further is to be done with these people?" For while they are working for our emancipation, we are, by our treachery, wickedness and deceit, working against ourselves and our children—helping ours, and the enemies of God, to keep us and our dear little children in their infernal chains of slavery!!! Indeed, our friends cannot but relapse and join themselves "with those who are actuated by *sordid avarice* only!!!"

For my own part, I am glad Mr. Jefferson has advanced his positions for your sake; for you will either have to contradict or confirm him by your own actions, and not by what our friends have said or done for us; for those things are other men's labours, and do not satisfy the Americans, who are waiting for us to prove to them ourselves, that we are MEN, before they will be willing to admit the fact; for I pledge you my sacred word of honour, that Mr. Jefferson's remarks respecting us, have sunk deep into the hearts of millions of the whites, and never will be removed this side of eternity.—

For how can they, when we are confirming him every day, by our *groveling submissions* and *treachery?* I aver, that when I look over these United States of America, and the world, and see the ignorant deceptions and consequent wretchedness of my brethren, I am brought oftimes solemnly to a stand, and in the midst of my reflections I exclaim to my God, "Lord didst thou make us to be slaves to our brethren, the whites?" But when I reflect that God is just, and that millions of my wretched brethren would meet death with glory—yea, more, would plunge into the very mouths of cannons and be torn into particles as minute as the atoms which compose the elements of the earth, in preference to a mean submission to the lash of tyrants, I am with streaming eyes, compelled to shrink back into nothingness before my Maker, and exclaim again, thy will be done, O Lord God Almighty.

Men of colour, who are also of sense, for you particularly is my APPEAL designed. Our more ignorant brethren are not able to penetrate its value. I call upon you therefore to cast your eyes upon the wretchedness of your brethren, and to do your utmost to enlighten them—*go to work and enlighten your brethren!*—Let the Lord see you doing what you can to rescue them and your selves from degradation. Do any of you say that you and your family are free and happy, and what have you to do with the wretched slaves and other people? So can I say, for I enjoy as much freedom as any of you, if I am not quite as well off as the best of you. Look into our freedom and happiness, and see of what kind they are composed!! They are of the very lowest kind—they are the very *dregs!*—they are the most servile and abject kind, that ever a people was in possession of! If any of you wish to know how FREE you are, let one of you start and go through the southern and western States of this country, and unless you travel as a slave to a white man (a servant is a slave to the man whom he serves) or have your free papers, (which if you are not careful they will get from you) if they do not take you up and put you in jail, and if you cannot give good evidence of your freedom, sell you into eternal slavery, I am not a living man: or any man of colour, immaterial who he is, or where he came from, if he is not *the fourth from the negro race!!* (as we are called) the white Christians of America will serve him the same they will sink him into wretchedness and degradation for ever while he lives. And yet some of you have the hardihood to say that you are free and happy! May God have mercy on your freedom and happiness!!

I met a coloured man in the street a short time since, with a string of boots on his shoulders; we fell into conversation, and in course of which, I said to him, what a miserable set of people we are! He asked, why?—Said I, we are so subjected under the whites, that we cannot obtain the comforts of life, but by cleaning their boots and shoes, old clothes, waiting on them, shaving them &c. Said he, (with the boots on his shoulders) "I am completely happy!!! I never want to live any better or happier than when I can get a plenty of boots and shoes to clean!!!" Oh! how can those who are actuated by avarice only, but think, that our Creator made us to be an inheritance to them for ever, when they see that our greatest glory is centered in such mean and low objects? Understand me, brethren, I do not mean to speak against the occupations by which we acquire enough and sometimes scarcely that, to render ourselves and families comfortable through life. I am subjected to the same inconvenience, as you all.—My objections are, to our *glorying* and being *happy* in such low employments; for if we are men, we ought to be thankful to the Lord for the past, and for the future. Be looking forward with thankful hearts to higher attainments than *wielding the razor* and *cleaning boots and shoes.* The man whose aspirations are not *above,* and even *below* these, is indeed, ignorant and wretched enough.

I advance it therefore to you, not as a *problematical,* but as an unshaken and for ever immoveable *fact,* that your full glory and happiness, as well as all other coloured people under Heaven, shall never be fully consummated, but with the *entire emancipation of your enslaved brethren all over*

93

the world. You may therefore, go to work and do what you can to rescue, or join in with tyrants to oppress them and yourselves, until the Lord shall come upon you all like a thief in the night. For I believe it is the will of the Lord that our greatest happiness shall consist in working for the salvation of our whole body. When this is accomplished a burst of glory will shine upon you, which will indeed astonish you and the world. Do any of you say this never will be done? I assure you that God will accomplish it—if nothing else will answer, he will hurl tyrants and devils into *atoms* and make way for his people. But O my brethren! I say unto you again, you must go to work and prepare the way of the Lord.

There is a great work for you to do, as trifling as some of you may think of it. You have to prove to the Americans and the world, that we are MEN, and not *brutes,* as we have been represented, and by millions treated. Remember, to let the aim of your labours among your brethren, and particularly the youths, be the dissemination of education and religion.* It is lamentable, that many of our children go to school, from four until they are eight or ten, and sometimes fifteen years of age, and leave school knowing but a little more about the grammar of their language than a horse does about handling a musket—and not a few of them are really so ignorant, that they are unable to answer a person correctly, general questions in geography, and to hear them read, would only be to disgust a man who has a taste for reading; which, to do well, as trifling as it may appear to

---

* Never mind what the ignorant ones among us may say, many of whom when you speak to them for their good, and try to enlighten their minds, laugh at you, and perhaps tell you plump to your face, that they want no instruction from you or any other Niger, and all such aggravating language. Now if you are a man of understanding and sound sense, I conjure you in the name of the Lord, and of all that is good, to impute their actions to ignorance, and wink at their follies, and do your very best to get around them some way or other, for remember they are your brethren; and I declare to you that it is for your interests to teach and enlighten them.

some, (to the ignorant in particular) is a great part of learning.

Some few of them, may make out to scribble tolerably well, over a half sheet of paper, which I believe has hitherto been a powerful obstacle in our way, to keep us from acquiring knowledge. An ignorant father, who knows no more than what nature has taught him, together with what little he acquires by the senses of hearing and seeing, finding his son able to write a neat hand, sets it down for granted that he has as good learning as any body; the young, ignorant gump, hearing his father or mother, who perhaps may be ten times more ignorant, in point of literature, than himself, extolling his learning, struts about, in the full assurance, that his attainments in literature are sufficient to take him through the world, when, in fact, he has scarcely any learning at all!!!!

I promiscuously fell in conversation once, with an elderly coloured man on the topics of education, and of the great prevalency of ignorance among us: Said he, "I know that our people are very ignorant but my son has a good education: I spent a great deal of money on his education: he can write as well as any white man, and I assure you that no one can fool him," &c. Said I, what else can your son do, besides writing a good hand? Can he post a set of books in a mercantile manner? Can he write a neat piece of composition in prose or in verse? To these interogations he answered in the negative. Said I, did your son learn, while he was at school, the width and depth of English Grammar? To which he also replied in the negative, telling me his son did not learn those things. Your son, said I, then has hardly any learning at all—he is almost as ignorant, and more so, than many of those who never went to school one day in all their lives. My friend got a little put out, and so walking off, said that his son could write as well as any white man. Most of the coloured people, when they speak of the education of one among us who can write a neat hand, and who perhaps knows nothing but to scribble and puff pretty fair on a small scrap of paper, immaterial whether his words are grammatical, or spelt correctly, or not; if it only looks beautiful, they say he has as good an education as any white man—he can write as well as any white man, &c. The poor, ignorant creature, hearing, this, he is ashamed, forever after, to let any person see him humbling himself to another for knowledge but going about trying to deceive those who are more ignorant than himself, he at last falls an ignorant victim to death in wretchedness.

I pray that the Lord may undeceive my ignorant brethren, and permit them to throw away pretensions, and seek after the substance of learning. I would crawl on my hands and knees through mud and mire, to the feet of a learned man, where I would sit and humbly supplicate him to instil into me, that which neither devils nor tyrants could remove, only with my life—for coloured people to acquire learning in this country, make tyrants quake and tremble on their sandy foundation. Why, what is the matter? Why, they know that their infernal deeds of cruelty will be made known to the world. Do you suppose one man of good sense and learning would submit himself, his father, mother, wife and children, to be slaves to a wretched man like himself, who, instead of compensating him for his labours, chains, hand-cuffs and beats him and family almost to death, leaving life enough in them, however, to work for, and call him master? No! no! he would cut his devilish throat from ear to ear, and well do slave-holders know it. The bare name of educating the coloured people, scares our cruel oppressors almost to death. But if they do not have enough to be frightened for yet, it will be, because they can always keep us ignorant, and because God approbates their cruelties, with which they have been for centuries murdering us. The whites shall have enough of the blacks, yet, as true as God sits on his throne in Heaven.

Some of our brethren are so very full of learning, that you cannot mention any thing to them which they do not know better than yourself!!—nothing is strange to them!!—they

knew every thing years ago!—if any thing should be mentioned in company where they are, immaterial how important it is respecting us or the world, if they had not divulged
it; they make light of it, and affect to have known it long
before it was mentioned and try to make all in the room,
or wherever you may be, believe that your conversation is
nothing!!—not worth hearing! All this is the result of ignorance and ill-breeding; for a man of good-breeding, sense
and penetration, if he had heard a subject told twenty times
over, and should happen to be in company where one should
commence telling it again, he would wait with patience on
its narrator, and see if he would tell it as it was told in his
presence before—paying the most strict attention to what is
said, to see if any more light will be thrown on the subject:
for all men are not gifted alike in telling, or even hearing the
most simple narration. These ignorant, vicious, and wretched
men, contribute almost as much injury to our body as
tyrants themselves, by doing so much for the promotion of
ignorance amongst us; for they, making such pretensions to
knowledge, such of our youth as are seeking after knowledge,
and can get access to them, take them as criterions to go by,
who will lead them into a channel, where, unless the Lord
blesses them with the privilege of seeing their folly, they will
be irretrievably lost forever, while in time!!!

I must close this article by relating the very heart-rending
fact, that I have examined school-boys and young men of
colour in different parts of the country, in the most simple
parts of Murray's English Grammar, and not more than one
in thirty was able to give a correct answer to my interroga-
tions. If anyone contradicts me, let him step out of his door
into the streets of Boston, New-York, Philadelphia, or Baltimore, (no use to mention any other, for the Christians are
too charitable further south or west!)—I say, let him who
disputes me, step out of his door into the streets of either of
those four cities, and promiscuously collect one hundred
school-boys, or young men of colour, *who have been to school,*

and who are considered by the coloured people to have received an excellent education, because, perhaps, some of them can write a good hand, but who, notwithstanding their neat writing, may be almost as ignorant, in comparison, as a horse.—And, I say it, he will hardly find (in this enlightened day, and in the midst of this *charitable* people) five in one hundred, who, are able to correct the false grammar of their language.—The cause of this almost universal ignorance among us, I appeal to our schoolmasters to declare.

Here is a fact, which I this very minute take from the mouth of a young coloured man, who has been to school in this state (Massachusetts) nearly nine years, and who knows grammar this day, *nearly* as well as he did the day he first entered the school-house, under a white master. This young man says: "My master would never allow me to study grammar." I asked him, why? "The school committee," said he "forbid the coloured children learning grammar—they would not allow any but the white children to study grammar." It is a notorious fact, that the major part of the white Americans, have, ever since we have been among them, tried to keep us ignorant, and make us believe that God made us and our children to be slaves to them and theirs. *Oh! my God, have mercy on Christian Americans!!!*

ARTICLE III.

OUR WRETCHEDNESS IN CONSEQUENCE OF THE PREACHERS OF THE RELIGION OF JESUS CHRIST

Religion, my brethren, is a substance of deep consideration among all nations of the earth. The Pagans have a kind, as well as the Mahometans, the Jews and the Christians. But pure and undefiled religion, such as was preached by Jesus Christ and his apostles, is hard to be found in all the earth. God, through his instrument, Moses, handed a dispensation of his Divine will, to the children of Israel after they had left Egypt for the land of Canaan or of Promise, who through hypocrisy, oppression and unbelief, departed from the faith.— He then, by his apostles, handed a dispensation of his, together with the will of Jesus Christ, to the Europeans in Europe, who, in open violation of which, have made *merchandise* of us, and it does appear as though they take this very dispensation to aid them in their *infernal* depredations upon us. Indeed, the way in which religion was and is conducted by the Europeans and their descendants, one might believe it was a plan fabricated by themselves and the *devils* to *oppress* us. But hark! My master has taught me better than to believe it—he has taught me that his gospel as it was preached by himself and his apostles remains the same, notwithstanding Europe has tried to mingle blood and oppression with it.

It is well known to the Christian world, that Bartholomew Las Casas, that very very notoriously avaricious Catholic priest or preacher, and adventurer with Columbus in his second voyage, proposed to his countrymen, the Spaniards in Hispaniola to import the Africans from the Portuguese settlement in Africa, to dig up gold and silver, and work their plantations for them, to effect which, he made a voyage thence to Spain, and opened the subject to his master, Ferdinand then in declining health, who listened to the plan: but who died soon after, and left it in the hand of his successor, Charles V.* This wretch, ("Las Casas, the Preacher,") succeeded so well in his plans of oppression, that in 1503, the first blacks had been imported into the new world. Elated with this success, and stimulated by sordid avarice only, he importuned Charles V. in 1511, to grant permission to a Flemish merchant to import 4000 blacks at one time.** Thus we see, through the instrumentality of a pretended preacher of the gospel of Jesus Christ our common master, our wretchedness first commenced in America—where it has been continued from 1503, to this day, 1829. A period of three hundred and twenty-six years. But two hundred and nine, from 1620—when twenty of our fathers were brought into Jamestown, Virginia, by a Dutch man of war, and sold off like brutes to the highest bidders; and there is not a doubt in my mind, but that tyrants are in hope to perpetuate our

* See Butler's History of the United States, vol. 1, page 24.— See also, page 25.

** It is not unworthy of remark, that the Portuguese and Spaniards, were among, if not the very first Nations upon Earth, about three hundred and fifty or sixty years ago—But see what those *Christians* have come to now in consequence of afflicting our fathers and us, who have never molested, or disturbed them or any other of the white *Christians,* but have they received one quarter of what the Lord will yet bring upon them, for the murders they have inflicted upon us?—They have had, and in some degree have now, sweet times on our blood and groans, the time however, of bitterness have sometime since commenced with them.—There is a God the Maker and preserver of all things, who will as sure as the world exists, give all his creatures their just recompense of reward in this and in the world to come, —we may fool or deceive, and keep each other in the most profound ignorance, beat murder and keep each other out of what is our lawful rights, or the rights of man, yet it is impossible for us to deceive or escape the Lord Almighty.

miseries under them and their children until the final consumation of all things.—But if they do not get dreadfully deceived, it will be because God has forgotten them.

The Pagans, Jews and Mahometans try to make proselytes to their religions, and whatever human beings adopt their religions they extend to them their protection. But Christian Americans, not only hinder their fellow creatures, the Africans, but thousands of them *will absolutely beat a coloured person nearly to death, if they catch him on his knees, supplicating the throne of grace.* This barbarous cruelty was by all the heathen nations of antiquity, and is by the Pagans, Jews and Mahometans of the present day, left entirely to Christian Americans to inflict on the Africans and their descendants, that their cup which is nearly full may be completed. I have known tyrants or usurpers of human liberty in different parts of this country to take their fellow creatures, the coloured people, and beat them until they would scarcely leave life in them; what for? Why they say "The black devils had the audacity to be found *making prayers and supplications to the God who made them!!!!"*

Yes, I have known small collections of coloured people to have convened together, for no other purpose than to worship God Almighty, in spirit and in truth, to the best of their knowledge; when tyrants, calling themselves *patrols,* would also convene and wait almost in breathless silence for the poor coloured people to commence singing and praying to the Lord our God, as soon as they had commenced, the wretches would burst in upon them and drag them out and commence beating them as they would rattle-snakes—many of whom, they would beat so unmercifully, that they would hardly be able to crawl for weeks and sometimes for months. Yet the American ministers send out missionaries to convert the heathen, while they keep us and our children sunk at their feet in the most abject ignorance and wretchedness that ever a people was afflicted with since the world began. Will the Lord suffer this people to proceed much longer? Will he

101

not stop them in their career? Does he regard the heathens abroad, more than the heathens among the Americans? Surely the Americans must believe that God is partial, notwithstanding his Apostle Peter, declared before Cornelius and others that he has no respect to persons, but in every nation he that feareth God and worketh righteousness is accepted with him. —"The word," said he, "which God sent unto the children of Israel, preaching peace, by Jesus Christ, (he is Lord of all."*) Have not the Americans the Bible in their hands? **Do** they believe it? Surely they do not. See how they treat us in open violation of the Bible!!

They no doubt will be greatly offended with me, but if God does not awaken them, it will be, because they are superior to other men, as they have represented themselves to be. Our divine Lord and Master said, "all things whatsoever ye would that men should do unto you, do ye even so unto them." But an American minister, with the Bible in his hand, holds us and our children in the most abject slavery and wretchedness. Now I ask them, would they like for us to hold them and their children in abject slavery and wrechedness? No says one, that never can be done—you are too abject and ignorant to do it—you are not men—you were made to be slaves to us, to dig up gold and silver for us and our children. Know this, my dear sirs, that although you treat us and our children now, as you do your domestic beast—yet the final result of all future events are known but to God Almighty alone, who rules in the armies of heaven and among the inhabitants of the earth, and who dethrones one earthly king and sits up another, as it seemeth good in his holy sight. We may attribute these vicissitudes to what we please, but the God of armies and of justice rules in heaven and in earth, and the whole American people shall see and know it yet, to their satisfaction.

I have known pretended preachers of the gospel of my

* See Acts of the Apostles, chap. xv.—25-27.

Master, who not only held us as their natural inheritance, but treated us with as much rigor as any Infidel or Deist in the world—just as though they were intent only on taking our blood and groans to glorify the Lord Jesus Christ. The wicked and ungodly, seeing their preachers treat us with so much cruelty, they say: our preachers, who must be right, if any body are, treat them like brutes, and why cannot we?— They think it is no harm to keep them in slavery and put the whip to them, and why cannot we do the same!—They being preachers of the gospel of Jesus Christ, if it were any harm, they would surely preach against their oppression and do their utmost to erase it from the country; not only in one or two cities, but one continual cry would be raised in all parts of this confederacy, and would cease only with the complete overthrow of the system of slavery, in every part of the country.

But how far the American preachers are from preaching against slavery and oppression, which have carried their country to the brink of a precipice; to save them from plunging down the side of which, will hardly be affected, will appear in the sequel of this paragraph, which I shall narrate just as it transpired. I remember a Camp Meeting in South Carolina, for which I embarked in a Steam Boat at Charleston, and having been five or six hours on the water, we at last arrived at the place of hearing, where was a very great concourse of people, who were no doubt, collected together to hear the word of God, (that some had collected barely as spectators to the scene, I will not here pretend to doubt, however, that is left to themselves and their God.)

Myself and boat companions, having been there a little while, we were all called up to hear; I among the rest went up and took my seat—being seated, I fixed myself in a complete position to hear the word of my Saviour and to receive such as I thought was authenticated by the Holy Scriptures; but to my no ordinary astonishment, our Reverend gentleman got up and told us (coloured people) that slaves must be obedient to their masters—must do their duty to their masters or be whipped—the whip was made for the backs of fools, &c. Here I pause for a moment, to give the world time to consider what was my surprise, to hear such preaching from a minister of my Master, whose very gospel is that of peace and not of blood and whips, as this pretended preacher tried to make us believe. What the American preachers can think of us, I aver this day before my God, I have never been able to define. They have newspapers and monthly periodicals, which they receive in continual succession, but on the pages of which, you will scarcely ever find a paragraph respecting slavery, which is ten thousand times more injurious to this country than all the other evils put together; and which will be the final overthrow of its government, unless something is very speedily done; for their cup is nearly full.—Perhaps they will laugh at or make light of this; but I tell you Americans! that unless you speedily alter your course, *you* and your *Country are gone!!!!!!* For God Almighty will tear up the very face of the earth!!!

Will not that very remarkable passage of Scripture be fulfilled on Christian Americans? Hear it Americans!! "He that is unjust, let him be unjust still:—and he which is filthy, let him be filthy still: and he that is righteous, let him be righteous still: and he that is holy, let him be holy still."* I hope that the Americans may hear, but I am afraid that they have done us so much injury, and are so firm in the belief that our Creator made us to be an inheritance to them for ever, that their hearts will be hardened, so that their destruction may be sure. This language, perhaps is too harsh for the American's delicate ears. But Oh Americans! Americans!! I warn you in the name of the Lord, (whether you will hear, or forbear,) to repent and reform, or you are ruined!!!

Do you think that our blood is hidden from the Lord,

* See Revelation, chap. xxii. II.

because you can hide it from the rest of the world, by sending our missionaries, and by your charitable deeds to the Greeks, Irish, &c? Will he not publish your secret crimes on the house top? Even here in Boston, pride and prejudice have got to such a pitch, that in the very houses erected to the Lord, they have built little places for the reception of coloured people, where they must sit during meeting, or keep away from the house of God, and the preachers say nothing about it—much less go into the hedges and highways seeking the lost sheep of the house of Israel, and try to bring them in to their Lord and Master. There are not a more wretched, ignorant, miserable, and abject set of beings in all the world, than the blacks in the Southern and Western sections of this country, under tyrants and devils. The preachers of America cannot see them, but they can send out missionaries to convert the heathens, notwithstanding. Americans! unless you speedily alter your course of proceeding, if God Almighty does not stop you, I say it in his name, that you may go on and do as you please for ever, both in time and eternity—never fear any evil at all!!!!!!!!

ADDITION.—The preachers and people of the United States form societies against Free Masonry and Intemperance, and write against Sabbath breaking, Sabbath mails, Infidelity, &c. &c. But the fountain head,* compared with which, all those other evils are comparatively nothing, and from the bloody and murderous head of which, they receive no trifling support, is hardly noticed by Americans. This is a fair illustration of the state of society in this country—it shows what a bearing *avarice* has upon a people, when they are nearly given up by the Lord to a hard heart and a reprobate mind, in consequence of afflicting their fellow creatures. God suffers some to go on until they are ruined for ever!!!!! Will it be the case with the whites of the United States of America?—We hope not—we would not wish to see them destroyed notwithstanding, they have and do now treat us

---

* Slavery and oppression.

more cruel than any people have treated another, on this earth since it came from the hands of its Creator (with the exceptions of the French and the Dutch, they treat us nearly as bad as the Americans of the United States.) The will of God must however, in spite of us, *be done.*

The English are the best friends the coloured people have upon earth. Though they have oppressed us a little and have colonies now in the West Indies, which oppress us *sorely.*— Yet notwithstanding they (the English) have done one hundred times more for the melioration of our condition, than all the other nations of the earth put together. The blacks cannot but respect the English as a nation, notwithstanding they have treated us a little cruel.

There is no intelligent *black man* who knows any thing, but esteems a real Englishman, let him see him in what part of the world he will—for they are the greatest benefactors we have upon earth. We have here and there, in other nations, good friends. But as a nation, the English are our friends.

How can the preachers and people of America believe the Bible? Does it teach them any distinction on account of man's colour? Hearken, Americans! to the injunctions of our Lord and Master, to his humble followers.

> * And Jesus came and spake unto them, saying all power is given unto me in Heaven and in earth.
>
> Go ye, therefore, and teach all nations, baptizing them in the name of the Father, and of the Son, and of the Holy Ghost.
>
> Teaching them to observe all things whatsoever I have commanded you; and lo, I am with you always, even unto the end of the world. Amen.

I declare, that the very face of these injunctions appear to be of God and not of man. They do not show the slightest degree of distinction. "Go ye therefore," (says my divine

* See St. Matthew's Gospel, chap. xxviii. 18, 19, 20. After Jesus was risen from the dead.

106

Master) "and teach all nations," (or in other words, all people) "baptizing them in the name of the Father, and of the Son, and of the Holy Ghost." Do you understand the above, Americans?

We are a people, notwithstanding many of you doubt it. You have the Bible in your hands, with this very injunction. —Have you been to Africa, teaching the inhabitants thereof the words of the Lord Jesus? "Baptizing them in the name of the Father, and of the Son, and of the Holy Ghost." Have you not, on the contrary, entered among us, and learnt us the art of throat-cutting, by setting us to fight, one against another, to take each other as prisoners of war, and sell to you for small bits of calicoes, old swords, knives, &c. to make slaves for you and your children? This being done, have you not brought us among you, in chains and hand-cuffs, like brutes, and treated us with all the cruelties and rigour your ingenuity could invent, consistent with the laws of your country, which (for the blacks) are tyrannical enough? Can the American preachers appeal unto God, the Maker and Searcher of hearts, and tell him, with the Bible in their hands, that they make no distinction on account of men's colour? Can they say, O God! thou knowest all things—thou knowest that we make no distinction between thy creatures, to whom we have to preach thy Word? Let them answer the Lord; and if they cannot do it in the affirmative, have they not departed from the Lord Jesus Christ, their master?

But some may say, that they never had, or were in possession of a religion, which made no distinction, and of course they could not have departed from it. I ask you then, in the name of the Lord, of what kind can your religion be? Can it be that which was preached by our Lord Jesus Christ from Heaven? I believe you cannot be so wicked as to tell him that his Gospel was that of *distinction*. What can the American preachers and people take God to be? Do they believe his words? If they do, do they believe that he will be mocked? Or do they believe, because they are whites and we blacks,

107

that God will have respect to them? Did not God make us all as it seemed best to himself? What right, then, has one of us, to despise another, and to treat him cruel, on account of his colour, which none, but the God who made it can alter? Can there be a greater absurdity in nature, and particularly in a free republican country?

But the Americans, having introduced slavery among them, their hearts have become almost seared, as with an hot iron, and God has nearly given them up to believe a lie in preference to the truth!!! And I am awfully afraid that pride, prejudice, avarice and blood, will, before long prove the final ruin of this happy republic, or land of *liberty!!!!* Can any thing be a greater mockery of religion than the way in which it is conducted by the Americans?

It appears as though they are bent only on daring God Almighty to do his best—they chain and handcuff us and our children and drive us around the country like brutes, and go into the house of the God of justice to return him thanks for having aided them in their infernal cruelties inflicted upon us. Will the Lord suffer this people to go on much longer, taking his holy name in vain? Will he not stop them, PREACHERS and all? O Americans! Americans!! I call God—I call angels—I call men, to witness, that your DE-STRUCTION *is at hand,* and will be speedily consummated unless you REPENT.

ARTICLE IV.

OUR WRETCHEDNESS IN CONSEQUENCE OF THE COLONIZING PLAN.

MY DEARLY BELOVED BRETHREN: This is a scheme on which so many able writers, together with that very judicious coloured Baltimorean, have commented, that I feel my delicacy about touching it. But as I am compelled to do the will of my Master, I declare, I will give you my sentiments upon it.—Previous, however, to giving my sentiments, either for or against it, I shall give that of Mr. Henry Clay, together with that of Mr. Elias B. Caldwell, Esq. of the District of Columbia, as extracted from the National Intelligencer, by Dr. Torrey, author of a series of "Essays on Morals, and the Diffusion of Useful Knowledge."

At a meeting which was convened in the District of Columbia, for the express purpose of agitating the subject of colonizing us in some part of the world, Mr. Clay was called to the chair, and having been seated a little while, he rose and spake, in substance, as follows: says he*—

> That class of the mixt population of our country [coloured people] was peculiarly situated; they neither enjoyed the immunities of freemen, nor were they subjected to the incapacities of slaves, but partook, in some degree, of the qualities of both. From their condition, and the unconquerable prejudices resulting from their colour, they never could amalgamate with the free whites of this country. It was desirable, therefore, as it respected them, and the resi-

---

* See Dr. Torrey's Portraiture of Domestic Slavery in the United States, page 85, 86.

due of the population of the country, to drain them off. Various schemes of colonization had been thought of, and a part of our continent, it was supposed by some, might furnish a suitable establishment for them. But, for his part, Mr. C. said, he had a decided preference for some part of the Coast of Africa. There ample provision might be made for the colony itself, and it might be rendered instrumental to the introduction into that extensive quarter of the globe, of the arts, civilization, and Christianity.

[Here I ask Mr. Clay, what kind of Christianity? Did he mean such as they have among the Americans—distinction, whip, blood and oppression? I pray the Lord Jesus Christ to forbid it.]
"There," said he,

was a peculiar, a moral fitness, in restoring them to the land of their fathers, and if instead of the evils and sufferings which we had been the innocent cause of inflicting upon the inhabitants of Africa, we can transmit to her the blessings of our arts, our civilization, and our religion. May we not hope that America will extinguish a great portion of that moral debt which she has contracted to that unfortunate continent? Can there be a nobler cause than that which, whilst it proposes, &c.***** [you know what this means.] contemplates the spreading of the arts of civilized life, and the possible redemption from ignorance and barbarism of a benighted quarter of the globe?

Before I proceed any further, I solicit your notice, brethren, to the foregoing part of Mr. Clay's speech, in which he says, (look above) "and if, instead of the evils and sufferings, which we had been the innocent cause of inflicting," &c. —What this very learned statesman could have been thinking about, when he said in his speech, "we had been the innocent cause of inflicting," &c., I have never been able to conceive. Are Mr. Clay and the rest of the Americans, innocent of the blood and groans of our fathers and us, their children?— Every individual may plead innocence, if he pleases, but

110

God will, before long, separate the innocent from the guilty, unless something is speedily done—which I suppose will hardly be, so that their destruction may be sure. Oh Americans! let me tell you, in the name of the Lord, it will be good for you, if you listen to the voice of the Holy Ghost, but if you do not, you are ruined!!! Some of you are good men; but the will of my God must be done. Those avaricious and ungodly tyrants among you, I am awfully afraid will drag down the vengeance of God upon you. When God Almighty commences his battle on the continent of America, for the oppression of his people, tyrants will wish they never were born.

But to return to Mr. Clay, whence I digressed. He says,

> It was proper and necessary distinctly to state, that he understood it constituted no part of the object of this meeting, to touch or agitate in the slightest degree, a delicate question, connected with another portion of the coloured population of our country. It was not proposed to deliberate upon or consider at all, any question of emancipation, or that which was connected with the abolition of slavery. It was upon that condition alone, he was sure, that many gentlemen from the South and the West, whom he saw present, had attended, or could be expected to co-operate. It was upon that condition only, that he himself had attended.

That is to say, to fix a plan to get those of the coloured people, who are said to be free, away from among those of our brethren whom they unjustly hold in bondage, so that they may be enabled to keep them the more secure in ignorance and wretchedness, to support them and their children, and consequently they would have the more obedient slave. For if the free are allowed to stay among the slave, they will have intercourse together, and, of course, the free will learn the slaves *bad habits*, by teaching them that they are MEN, as well as other people, and certainly *ought* and *must* be FREE.

I presume, that every intelligent man of colour must have

some idea of Mr. Henry Clay, originally of Virginia, but now of Kentucky; they know too, perhaps, whether he is a friend, or a foe to the coloured citizens of this country, and of the world. This gentleman, according to his own words, had been highly favoured and blessed of the Lord, though he did not acknowledge it; but, to the contrary, he acknowledged men, for all the blessings with which God had favoured him. At a public dinner, given him at Fowler's Garden, Lexington, Kentucky, he delivered a public speech to a very large concourse of people—in the concluding clause of which, he says,

And now, my friends and fellow citizens, I cannot part from you, on possibly the last occasion of my ever publicly addressing you, without reiterating the expression of my thanks, from a heart overflowing with gratitude. I came among you, now more than thirty years ago, an orphan boy, pennyless, a stranger to you all, without friends, without the favour of the great, you took me up, cherished me, protected me, honoured me, you have constantly poured upon me a bold and unabated stream of innumerable favours, time which wears out every thing has increased and strengthened your affection for me. When I seemed deserted by almost the whole world, and assailed by almost every tongue, and pen, and press, you have fearlessly and manfully stood by me, with unsurpassed zeal and undiminished friendship. When I felt as if I should sink beneath the storm of abuse and detraction, which was violently raging around me, I have found myself upheld and sustained by your encouraging voices and approving smiles. I have doubtless, committed many faults and indiscretions, over which you have thrown the broad mantle of your charity. But I can say, and in the presence of God and in this assembled multitude, I will say, that I have honestly and faithfully served my country—that I have never wronged it—and that, however unprepared, I lament that I am to appear in the Divine presence on other accounts, I invoke the stern justice of his judgment on my public conduct, without the slightest apprehension of his displeasure.

Hearken to this Statesman indeed, but no philanthropist, whom God sent into Kentucky, an orphan boy, pennyless, and friendless, where he not only gave him a plenty of friends and the comforts of life, but raised him almost to the very highest honour in the nation, where his great talents, with which the Lord has been pleased to bless him, has gained for him the affection of a great portion of the people with whom he had to do. But what has this gentleman done for the Lord, after having done so much for him? The Lord has a suffering people, whose moans and groans at his feet for deliverance from oppression and wretchedness, pierce the very throne of Heaven, and call loudly on the God of Justice, to be revenged. Now, what this gentleman, who is so highly favoured of the Lord, has done to liberate those miserable victims of oppression, shall appear before the world, by his letters to Mr. Gallatin, Envoy Extraordinary and Minister Plenipotentiary to Great Britain, dated June 19, 1826.—Though Mr. Clay was writing for the States, yet nevertheless, it appears, from the very face of his letters to that gentleman, that he was as anxious, if not more so, to get those free people and sink them into wretchedness, as his constituents, for whom he wrote.

The Americans of North and of South America, including the West India Islands—no trifling portion of whom were, for stealing, murdering, &c. compelled to flee from Europe, to save their necks or banishment, have effected their escape to this continent, where God blessed them with all the comforts of life—He gave them a plenty of every thing calculated to do them good—not satisfied with this, however, they wanted slaves, and wanted us for their slaves, who belong to the Holy Ghost, and no other, who we shall have to serve instead of tyrants.—I say, the Americans want us, the property of the Holy Ghost, to serve them.

But there is a day fast approaching, when (unless there is a universal repentance on the part of the whites, which will scarcely take place, they have got to be hardened in consequence of our blood, and so wise in their own conceit.) To be plain and candid with you, Americans! I say that the day is fast approaching, when there will be a greater time on the continent of America, than ever was witnessed upon this earth, since it came from the hand of its Creator. Some of you have done us so much injury, that you will never be able to repent.—Your cup must be filled.—You want us for your slaves, and shall have enough of us—God is just, *who will give you your fill of us.* But Mr. Henry Clay, speaking to Mr. Gallatin, respecting coloured people, who had effected their escape from the U. States (or to them *hell upon earth!!!*) to the hospitable shores of Canada,* from whence it would cause more than the lives of the Americans to get them, to plunge into wretchedness—he says:

> The General Assembly of Kentucky, one of the states which is most affected by the escape of slaves into Upper Canada, has again, at their session which has just terminated, invoked the interposition of the General Government. In the treaty which has been recently concluded with the United Mexican States, and which is now under the consideration of the Senate, provision is made for the restoration of fugitive slaves. As it appears from your statements of what passed on that subject, with the British Plenipotentiaries, that they admitted the correctness of the principle of restoration, it is hoped that you will be able to succeed in making satisfactory arrangements.

There are a series of these letters, all of which are to the same amount; some however, presenting a face more of his own responsibility. I wonder what would this gentleman think, if the Lord should give him among the rest of his blessings enough of slaves? Could he blame any other being but himself? Do we not belong to the Holy Ghost. What business has he or any body else, to be sending letters about the world respecting us? Can we not go where we want to, as

* Among the English, our real friends and benefactors.

well as other people, only if we obey the voice of the Holy
Ghost? This gentleman, (Mr. Henry Clay) not only took an
active part in this colonizing plan, but was absolutely chairman of a meeting held at Washington, the 21st day of December 1816,* to agitate the subject of colonizing us in
Africa.—Now I appeal and ask every citizen of these United
States and of the world, both *white* and *black,* who has any
knowledge of Mr. Clay's public labor for these States—I want
you candidly to answer the Lord, who sees the secrets of
our hearts.—Do you believe that Mr. Henry Clay, late Secretary of State, and now in Kentucky, is a friend to the blacks,
further, than his personal interest extends? Is it not his
greatest object and glory upon earth, to sink us into miseries
and wretchedness by making slaves of us, to work his plantation to enrich him and his family? Does he care a pinch of
snuff about Africa—whether it remains a land of Pagans and
of blood, or of Christians, so long as he get enough of her
sons and daughters to dig up gold and silver for him? If he
had no slaves, and could obtain them in no other way if it
were not, repugnant to the laws of his country, which prohibit
the importation of slaves (which act was, indeed, more
through apprehension than humanity) would he not try to
import a few from Africa, to work his farm? Would he work
in the hot sun to earn his bread, if he could make an African
work for nothing, particularly, if he could keep him in ignorance and make him believe that God made him for nothing
else but to work for him? Is not Mr. Clay a white man, and
too delicate to work in the hot sun!! Was he not made by his
Creator to sit in the shade, and make the blacks work without
remuneration for their services, to support him and his
family!!!

I have been for some time taking notice of this man's
speeches and public writings, but never to my knowledge
have I seen any thing in his writings which insisted on the

* In the first edition of this work, it should read 1816, as above, and not
1826, as it there appears.

emancipation of slavery, which has almost ruined his country. Thus we see the depravity of men's hearts, when in pursuit only of gain—particularly when they oppress their fellow creatures to obtain that gain—God suffers some to go on until they are lost forever. This same Mr. Clay, wants to know, what he has done, to merit the disapprobation of the American people. In a public speech delivered by him, he asked: "Did I involve my country in an unnecessary war?" to merit the censure of the Americans—"Did I bring obliquy upon the nation, or the people whom I represented—did I ever lose any opportunity to advance the fame, honor and prosperity of this State and the Union?" How astonishing it is, for a man who knows so much about God and his ways, as Mr. Clay, to ask such frivolous questions? Does he believe that a man of his talents and standing in the midst of a people, will get along unnoticed by the penetrating and all seeing eye of God, who is continually taking cognizance of the hearts of men? Is not God against him, for advocating the murderous cause of slavery? If God is against him, what can the Americans, together with the whole world do for him? Can they save him from the hand of the Lord Jesus Christ?

I shall now pass in review the speech of Mr. Elias B. Caldwell, Esq. of the District of Columbia, extracted from the same page on which Mr. Clay's will be found. Mr. Caldwell, giving his opinion respecting us, at that ever memorable meeting, he says: "The more you improve the condition of these people, the more you cultivate their minds, the more miserable you make them in their present state. You give them a higher relish for those privileges which they can never attain, and turn what we intend for a blessing into a curse." Let me ask this benevolent man, what he means by a blessing intended for us? Did he mean sinking us and our children into ignorance and wretchedness, to support him and his family? What he meant will appear evident and obvious to the most ignorant in the world. See Mr. Caldwell's intended blessings for us, O! my Lord!! "No," said he, "if they must remain in their present situation, keep them in the *lowest state of degradation and ignorance.* The nearer you bring them to the condition of brutes, the better chance do you give them of possessing their *apathy."*

Here I pause to get breath, having labored to extract the above clause of this gentleman's speech, at that colonizing meeting. I presume that everybody knows the meaning of the word "apathy,"—if any do not, let him get Sheridan's Dictionary, in which he will find it explained in full. I solicit the attention of the world, to the foregoing part of Mr. Caldwell's speech, that they may see what man will do with his fellow men, when he has them under his feet. To what length will not man go in iniquity when given up to a hard heart, and reprobate mind, in consequence of blood and oppression? The last clause of this speech, which was written in a very artful manner, and which will be taken for the speech of a friend, without close examination and deep penetration, I shall now present. He says, "surely, Americans ought to be the last people on earth, to advocate such slavish doctrines, to cry peace and contentment to those who are deprived of the privileges of civil liberty, they who have so largely partaken of its blessings, who know so well how to estimate its value, ought to be among the foremost to extend it to others." The real sense and meaning of the last part of Mr. Caldwell's speech is, get the free people of colour away to Africa, from among the slaves, where they may at once be blessed and happy, and those who we hold in slavery, will be contented to rest in ignorance and wretchedness, to dig up gold and silver for us and our children. Men have indeed got to be so cunning, these days, that it would take the eye of a Solomon to penetrate and find them out.

ADDITION.—Our dear Redeemer said, "Therefore, whatsoever ye have spoken in darkness, shall be heard in the light; and that which ye have spoken in the ear in closets, shall be proclaimed upon the house tops."

How obviously this declaration of our Lord has been

117

shown among the Americans of the United States. They have hitherto passed among some nations, who do not know any thing about their internal concerns, for the most enlightened, humane, charitable, and merciful people upon earth, when at the same time they treat us, the (coloured people) secretly more cruel and unmerciful than any other nation upon earth.

It is a fact, that in our Southern and Western States, there are millions who hold us in chains or in slavery, whose greatest object and glory is, centered in keeping us sunk in the most profound ignorance and stupidity, to make us work without remunerations for our services. Many of whom if they catch a coloured person, whom they hold in unjust ignorance, slavery and degradation, to them and their children, with a book in his hand, will beat him nearly to death. I heard a wretch in the state of North Carolina said, that if any man would teach a black person whom he held in slavery, to spell, read or write, he would prosecute him to the very extent of the law.—Said the ignorant wretch,* "a Nigar, ought not to have any more sense than enough to work for his master." May I not ask to fatten the wretch and his family?—These and similar cruelties these *Christians* have been for hundreds of years inflicting on our fathers and us in the dark, God has however, very recently published some of their secret crimes on the house top, that the world may gaze on their Christianity and see of what kind it is composed.

Georgia for instance, God has completely shown to the world, the *Christianity* among its white *inhabitants.* A law has recently passed the Legislature of this *republican* State (Georgia) prohibiting all free or slave persons of colour, from learning to read or write; another law has passed the *republican* House of Delegates, (but not the Senate) in

* It is a fact, that in all our Slave-holding States (in the countries) there are thousands of the whites, who are almost as ignorant in comparison as horses, the most they know, is to beat the coloured people, which some of them shall have their hearts full of yet.

118

Virginia, to prohibit all persons of colour, (free and slave) from learning to read or write, and even to hinder them from meeting together in order to worship our Maker!!!!!!— Now I solemly appeal, to the most skilful historians in the world, and all those who are mostly acquainted with the histories of the Antideluvians and of Sodom and Gomorrah, to show me a parallel of barbarity. *Christians!! Christians!!!* I dare you to show me a parallel of cruelties in the annals of Heathens or of Devils, with those of Ohio, Virginia and of Georgia—know the world that these things were before done in the dark, or in a corner under a garb of humanity and religion. God has however, taken off the fig-leaf covering and make them expose themselves on the house top. I tell you that God works in many ways his wonders to perform, he will unless they repent, make them expose themselves enough more yet to the world.—See the acts of the *Christians* in FLORIDA, SOUTH CAROLINA, and KENTUCKY— was it not for the reputation of the house of my Lord and Master, I would mention here, an act of cruelty inflicted a few days since on a black man, by the white *Christians* in the PARK STREET CHURCH, in this (CITY) which is almost enough to make Demons themselves quake and tremble in their FIERY HABITATIONS.—Oh! my Lord how refined in iniquity the whites have got to be in consequence of our blood*—what kind!! Oh! what kind!!! of Christianity can be found this day in all the earth!!!!!!

I write without the fear of man, I am writing for my God, and fear none but himself; they may put me to death if they choose—(I fear and esteem a good man however, let him be black or white.) I forbear to comment on the cruelties inflicted on this Black Man by the Whites, in the Park Street MEETING HOUSE, I will leave it in the dark!!!!! But I declare that the atrocity is really to Heaven daring and

---

* The Blood of our fathers who have been murdered by the whites, and the groans of our Brethren, who are now held in cruel ignorance, wretchedness and slavery by them, cry aloud to the Maker of Heaven and of earth, against the whole continent of America, for redresses.

infernal, that I must say that God has commenced a course of exposition among the Americans, and the glorious and heavenly work will continue to progress until they learn to do justice.

Extract from the Speech of Mr. John Randolph, of Roanoke.
Said he:—

It had been properly observed by the Chairman, as well as by the gentleman from this District [meaning Messrs. Clay and Caldwell] that there was nothing in the proposition submitted to consideration which in the smallest degree touches another very important and delicate question, which ought to be left as much out of view as possible, [Negro Slavery.]*

There is no fear, [Mr. R. said] that this proposition would alarm the slave-holders; they had been accustomed to think seriously of the subject.—There was a popular work on agriculture, by John Taylor of Caroline, which was widely circulated, and much confided in, in Virginia. In that book, much read because coming from a practical man, this description of people [referring to us half free ones] were pointed out as a great evil. They had indeed been held up as the greater bug-bear to every man who feels an inclination to emancipate his slaves, not to create in the bosom of his country so great a nuisance. If a place could be provided for their reception, and a mode of sending them hence, there were hundreds, nay thousands of citizens who would, by manumitting their slaves, relieve themselves from the cares attendant on their possession. The great slave-holder, [Mr. R. said,] was frequently a mere

---

* "Niger," is a word derived from the Latin, which was used by the old Romans, to designate inanimate beings, which were black; such as soot, pot, wood, house, &c. Also, animals which they considered inferior to the human species, as a black horse, cow, hog, bird, dog, &c. The white Americans have applied this term to Africans, by way of reproach for our colour, to aggravate and heighten our miseries, because they have their feet on our throats.

120

sentry at his own door—bound to stay on his plantation to see that his slaves were properly treated, &c. [Mr. R. concluded by saying,] that he had thought it necessary to make these remarks being a slave-holder himself, to shew that, so far from being connected with abolition of slavery, the measure proposed would prove one of the greatest securities to enable the master to keep in possession his own property.

Here is a demonstrative proof, of a plan got up, by a gang of slave-holders to select the free people of colour from among the slaves, that our more miserable brethren may be the better secured in ignorance and wretchedness, to work their farms and dig their mines, and thus go on enriching the Christians with their blood and groans. What our brethren could have been thinking about, who have left their native land and home and gone away to Africa, I am unable to say. This country is as much ours as it is the whites, whether they will admit it now or not, they will see and believe it by and by. They tell us about prejudices—what have we to do with it? Their prejudices will be obliged to fall like lightning to the ground, in succeeding generations; not, however, with the will and consent of all the whites, for some will be obliged to hold on to the old adage, viz: the blacks are not men, but were made to be an inheritance to us and our children for ever!!!!!! I hope the residue of the coloured people, will stand still and see the salvation of God and the miracle which he will work for our delivery from wretchedness under the Christians!!!!!!
ADDITION.—If any of us see fit to go away, go to those who have been for many years, and are now our greatest earthly friends and benefactors—the English. If not so, go to our brethren, the Haytians, who, according to their word, are bound to protect and comfort us. The Americans say, that we are ungrateful—but I ask them for heaven's sake, what should we be grateful to them for—for murdering our fathers and mothers?—Or do they wish us to return thanks to them for chaining and hand-cuffing us, branding us,

cramming fire down our throats, or for keeping us in slavery, and beating us nearly or quite to death to make us work in ignorance and miseries, to support them and their families. They certainly think that we are a gang of fools. Those among them, who have volunteered their services for our redemption, though we are unable to compensate them for their labours, we nevertheless thank them from the bottom of our hearts, and have our eyes steadfastly fixed upon them, and their labours of love for God and man.—But do slaveholders think that we thank them for keeping us in miseries, and taking our lives by the inches?

Before I proceed further with this scheme, I shall give an extract from the letter of that truly Reverent Divine, (Bishop Allen,) of Philadelphia, respecting this trick. At the instance of the editor of the Freedom's Journal, he says,

> Dear Sir, I have been for several years trying to reconcile my mind to the Colonizing of Africans in Liberia, but there have always been, and there still remain great and insurmountable objections against the scheme. We are an unlettered people, brought up in ignorance, not one in a hundred can read or write, not one in a thousand has a liberal education; is there any fitness for such to be sent into a far country, among heathens, to convert or civilize them, when they themselves are neither civilized or Christianized? See the great bulk of the poor, ignorant Africans in this country, exposed to every temptation before them: all for the want of their morals being refined by education and proper attendance paid unto them by their owners, or those who had the charge of them. It is said by the Southern slave-holders, that the more ignorant they can bring up the Africans, the better slaves they make, ["go and come."] Is there any fitness for such people to be colonized in a far country to be their own rulers? Can we not discern the project of sending the free people of colour away from their country? Is it not for the interest of the slave-holders to select the free people of colour out of the different states, and send them to Liberia? Will it not make their slaves uneasy to see free men of colour enjoying liberty? It is

against the law in some of the Southern States, that a person of colour should receive an education, under a severe penalty. Colonizationists speak of America being first colonized; but is there any comparison between the two? America was colonized by as *wise, judicious* and *educated* men as the world afforded. WILLIAM PENN did not want for *learning, wisdom,* or *intelligence.* If all the people were as ignorant and in the same situation as our brethren, what would become of the world? Where would be the principle or piety that would govern the people? We were *stolen* from our mother country, and brought *here.* We have *tilled* the ground and made fortunes for thousands, and still they are not weary of our services. *But they who stay to till the ground must be slaves.* Is there not land enough in America, or "corn enough in Egypt?" Why should they send us into a far country to die? See the thousands of foreigners emigrating to America every year: and if there be ground sufficient for them to cultivate, and bread for them to eat, why would they wish to send the *first tillers* of the land away? Africans have made fortunes for thousands, who are yet unwilling to part with their services; but the free must be sent away, and those who remain, must be *slaves.* I have no doubt that there are many good men who do not see as I do, and who are sending us to Liberia; but they have not duly considered the subject—they are not men of colour.—This land which we have watered with our *tears* and *our blood,* is now our *mother country,* and we are well satisfied to stay where wisdom abounds and the gospel is free.

RICHARD ALLEN,
Bishop of the African Methodist Episcopal
Church in the United States*

I have given you, my brethren, an extract verbatim, from the letter of that godly man, as you may find it on the aforementioned page of Freedom's Journal. I know that thousands, and perhaps millions of my brethren in these States, have never heard of such a man as Bishop Allen—a man

---

* See Freedom's Journal for Nov. 2d, 1827—vol. 1, No. 34.

whom God many years ago raised up among his ignorant and degraded brethren, to preach Jesus Christ and him crucified to them—who notwithstanding, had to wrestle against principalities and the powers of darkness to diffuse that gospel with which he was endowed among his brethren—but who having overcome the combined powers of devils and wicked men, has under God planted a Church among us which will be as durable as the foundation of the earth on which it stands. Richard Allen! O my God!! The bare recollection of the labours of this man, and his ministers among his deplorably wretched brethren, (rendered so by the whites) to bring them to a knowledge of the God of Heaven, fills my soul with all those very high emotions which would take the pen of an Addison to portray.

It is impossible my brethren for me to say much in this work respecting that man of God. When the Lord shall raise up coloured historians in succeeding generations, to present the crimes of this nation, to the then gazing world, the Holy Ghost will make them do justice to the name of Bishop Allen, of Philadelphia. Suffice it for me to say, that the name of this very man (Richard Allen) though now in obscurity and degradation, will notwithstanding, stand on the pages of history among the greatest divines who have lived since the apostolic age, and among the Africans, Bishop Allen's will be entirely pre-eminent. My brethren, search after the character and exploits of this godly man among his ignorant and miserable brethren, to bring them to a knowledge of the truth as it is in our Master. Consider upon the tyrants and false Christians against whom he had to contend in order to get access to his brethren. See him and his ministers in the States of New York, New Jersey, Pennsylvania, Delaware and Maryland, carrying the gladsome tidings of free and full salvation to the coloured people.

Tyrants and false Christians however, would not allow him to penetrate far into the South, for fear that he would awaken some of his ignorant brethren, whom they held in wretchedness and misery—for fear, I say it, that he would awaken and bring them to a knowledge of their Maker. O my Master! my Master! I cannot but think upon Christian Americans!!!—What kind of people can they be? Will not those who were burnt up in Sodom and Gomorrah rise up in judgment against Christian Americans with the Bible in their hands, and condemn them? Will not the Scribes and Pharisees of Jerusalem, who had nothing but the laws of Moses and the Prophets to go by, rise up in judgment against Christian Americans and condemn them,* who, in addition to these have a revelation from Jesus Christ the Son of the Living God?

In fine, will not the Antideluvians, together with the whole heathen world of antiquity, rise up in judgment against Christian Americans and condemn them? The Christians of Europe and America go to Africa, bring us away, and throw us into the seas, and in other ways murder us, as they would wild beasts. The Antideluvians and heathens never dreamed of such barbarities.—Now the Christians believe, because they have a name to live, while they are dead, that God will overlook such things. But if he does not deceive them, it will be because he has overlooked it sure enough.

But to return to this godly man, Bishop Allen. I do hereby openly affirm it to the world, that he has done more in a spiritual sense for his ignorant and wretched brethren than any other man of colour has, since the world began. And as for the greater part of the whites, it has hitherto been their greatest object and glory to keep us ignorant of our Maker, so as to make us believe that we were made to be slaves to them and their children, to dig up gold and silver for them. It is notorious that not a few professing Christians among the whites, who profess to love our Lord and Saviour Jesus Christ, have assailed this man and laid all the obstacles in his way they possibly could, consistent with their profession

* I mean those whose labours for the good, or rather destruction of Jerusalem, and the Jews. Ceased before our Lord entered the Temple, and overturned the tables of the Money Changers.

125

—and what for? Why, their course of proceeding and his, clashed exactly together—they trying their best to keep us ignorant, that we might be the better and more obedient slaves—while he, on the other hand, doing his very best to enlighten us and teach us a knowledge of the Lord.

And I am sorry that I have it to say, that many of our brethren have joined in with our oppressors, whose dearest objects are only to keep us ignorant and miserable against this man to stay his hand.—However, they have kept us in so much ignorance, that many of us know no better than to fight against ourselves, and by that means strengthen the hands of our natural enemies, to rivet their infernal chains of slavery upon us and our children. I have several times called the white Americans our *natural enemies*—I shall here define my meaning of the phrase. Shem, Ham and Japheth, together with their father Noah and wives, I believe were not natural enemies to each other. When the ark rested after the flood upon Mount Arrarat, in Asia, they (eight) were all the people which could be found alive in all the earth—in fact if Scriptures be true, (which I believe are) there were no other living men in all the earth, notwithstanding some ignorant creatures hesitate not to tell us that we, (the blacks) are the seed of Cain the murderer of his brother Abel.

But where or of whom those ignorant and avaricious wretches could have got their information, I am unable to declare. Did they receive it from the Bible? I have searched the Bible as well as they, if I am not as well learned as they are, and have never seen a verse which testifies whether we are the seed of Cain or of Abel. Yet those men tell us that we are the seed of Cain, and that God put a dark stain upon us, that we might be known as their slaves!!! Now, I ask those avaricious and ignorant wretches, who act more like the seed of Cain, by murdering the whites or the blacks? How many vessel loads of human beings, have the blacks thrown into the seas? How many thousand souls have the blacks murdered in cold blood, to make them work in

126

wretchedness and ignorance, to support them and their families?*

However, let us be the seed of *Cain, Harry, Dick,* or *Tom!!!* God will show the whites what we are, yet. I say, from the beginning, I do not think that we were natural enemies to each other. But the whites having made us so wretched, by subjecting us to slavery, and having murdered so many millions of us, in order to make us work for them, and out of devilishness—and they taking our wives, whom we love as we do ourselves—our mothers, who bore the pains of death to give us birth—our fathers and dear little children, and ourselves, and strip and beat us one before the other— chain, hand-cuff, and drag us about like rattle-snakes—shoot us down like wild bears, before each other's faces, to make us submissive to, and work to support them and their fami- lies. They (the whites) know well, if we are *men*—and there is a secret monitor in their hearts which tells them we are —they know, I say, if we *are* men, and see them treating us in the manner they do, that there can be nothing in our hearts but death alone, for them, notwithstanding we may appear cheerful, when we see them murdering our dear mothers and wives, because we cannot help ourselves.

Man, in all ages and all nations of the earth, is the same. Man is a peculiar creature—he is the image of his God, though he may be subjected to the most wretched condition upon earth, yet the spirit and feeling which constitute the creature, man, can never be entirely erased from his breast, because God who made him after his own image, planted it in his heart; he cannot get rid of it. The whites knowing this, they do not know what to do; they know that they have done us so much injury, they are afraid that we, being men, and not brutes, will retaliate, and woe will be to them;

* How many millions souls of the human family have the blacks beat nearly to death, to keep them from learning to read the Word of God, and from writing. And telling lies about them, by holding them up to the world as a tribe of TALKING APES, void of INTELLECT!!! *incapable* of LEARN- ING, &c.

therefore, that dreadful fear, together with an avaricious spirit, and the natural love in them, to be called masters, (which term will yet honour them with to their sorrow) bring them to the resolve that they will keep us in ignorance and wretchedness, as long as they possibly can,* and make the best of their time, while it lasts. Consequently they, themselves, (and not us) render themselves our natural enemies, by treating us so cruel.

They keep us miserable now, and call us their property, but some of them will have enough of us by and by—their stomachs shall run over with us; they want us for their slaves, and shall have us to their fill. (We are all in the world together!!—I said above, because we cannot help ourselves, (viz. we cannot help the whites murdering our mothers and our wives) but this statement is incorrect—for we can help ourselves; for, if we lay aside abject servility, and be determined to act like men, and not brutes—the murderers among the whites would be afraid to show their cruel heads. But O, my God!—in sorrow I must say it, that my colour, all over the world, have a mean, servile spirit. They yield in a moment to the whites, let them be right or wrong—the reason they are able to keep their feet on our throats. Oh! my coloured brethren, all over the world, when shall we arise from this death-like apathy?—And be men!! You will notice, if ever we become men, (I mean *respectable*

* And still hold us up with indignity as being incapable of acquiring knowledge!!! See the inconsistency of the assertions of those wretches—they beat us inhumanely, sometimes almost to death, for attempting to inform ourselves, by reading the *Word* of our Maker, and at the same time tell us, that we are beings *void of intellect*!!! How admirably their practices agree with their professions in this case. Let me cry shame upon you Americans, for such outrages upon human nature!!! If it were possible for the whites always to keep us ignorant and miserable, and make us work to enrich them and their children, and insult our feelings by representing us as *talking Apes*, what would they do? But glory, honour and praise to Heaven's King, that the sons and daughters of Africa, will, in spite of all the opposition of their enemies, stand forth in all the dignity and glory that is granted by the Lord to his creature man.

men, such as other people are,) we must exert ourselves to the full.

For remember, that it is the greatest desire and object of the greater part of the whites, to keep us ignorant, and make us work to support them and their families.—Here now, in the Southern and Western sections of this country, there are at least three coloured persons for one white, why is it, that those few weak, good-for-nothing whites, are able to keep so many able men, one of whom, can put to flight a dozen whites, in wretchedness and misery? It shows at once, what the blacks are, we are ignorant, abject, servile and mean—and the whites know it—they know that we are too servile to assert our rights as men—or they would not fool with us as they do. Would they fool with any other people as they do with us? No, they know too well, that they would get themselves ruined. Why do they not bring the inhabitants of Asia to be body servants to them? They know they would get their bodies rent and torn from head to foot. Why do they not get the Aborigines of this country to be slaves to them and their children, to work their farms and dig their mines? They know well that the Aborigines of this country, or (Indians) would tear them from the earth. The Indians would not rest day or night, they would be up all times of the night, cutting their cruel throats. But my colour, (some, not all,) are willing to stand still and be murdered by the cruel whites. In some of the West-India Islands, and over a large part of South America, there are six or eight coloured persons for one white.* Why do they not take possession of those places? Who hinders them? It is not the avaricious whites

* For instance in the two States of Georgia, and South Carolina, there are, perhaps, not much short of six or seven hundred thousand persons of colour; and if I was a gambling character, I would not be afraid to stake down upon the board FIVE CENTS against TEN, that there are in the single State of Virginia, five or six hundred thousand Coloured persons. Four hundred and fifty thousand of whom (let them be well equipt for war) I would put against every white person on the whole continent of America. (Why? Why because I know that the Blacks, once they get involved in a war, had rather die than to live, they either kill or be killed.) The whites know this too, which make

—for they are too busily engaged in laying up money—derived from the blood and tears of the blacks. The fact is, they are too servile, they love to have Masters too well!!

Some of our brethren, too, who seeking more after self aggrandisement, than the glory of God, and the welfare of their brethren, join in with our oppressors, to ridicule and say all manner of evils falsely against our Bishop. They think, that they are doing great things, when they can get in company with the whites, to ridicule and make sport of those who are labouring for their good. Poor ignorant creatures, they do not know that the sole aim and object of the whites, are only to make fools and slaves of them, and put the whip to them, and make them work to support them and their families.

But I do say, that no man, can well be a despiser of Bishop Allen, for his public labours among us, unless he is a despiser of God and of Righteousness. Thus, we see, my brethren, the two very opposite positions of those great men, who have written respecting this "Colonizing Plan." (Mr. Clay and

---

them quake and tremble. To show the world further, how servile the coloured people are, I will only hold up to view, the one Island of Jamaica, as a specimen of our meanness.

In that Island, there are three hundred and fifty thousand souls—of whom fifteen thousand are whites, the remainder, three hundred and thirty-five thousand are coloured people and this Island is ruled by the white people!!! (15,000) ruling and tyranizing over 335,000 persons!—O! coloured men! O! coloured men!! O! coloured men!! Look!! look!! at this!! and, tell me if we are not abject and servile enough, how long, O! how long my colour shall we be dupes and dogs to the cruel whites?—I only passed Jamaica, and its inhabitants, in review as a specimen to show the world, the condition of the Blacks at this time, now coloured people of the whole world, I beg you to look at the (15000 white,) and (Three Hundred and Thirty-five Thousand coloured people) in that Island, and tell me how can the white tyrants of the world but say that we are not men, but were made to be slaves and Dogs to them and their children forever!!!—why my friends only look at the thing!!! (15000) whites keeping in wretchedness and degradation (335000) viz. 22 coloured persons for one white!!!) when at the same time, an equal number (15000) Blacks would almost take the whole of South America, because where they go as soldiers to fight death follows in their train.

his slave-holding party,) men who are resolved to keep us in
people are, I will only hold up to view, the one Island of Jamacia, as a
eternal wretchedness, are also bent upon sending us to
Liberia. While the Reverend Bishop Allen, and his party,
men who have the fear of God, and the welfare of their
brethren at heart. The Bishop, in particular, whose labours
for the salvation of his brethren, are well known to a large
part of those, who dwell in the United States, are completely
opposed to the plan—and advise us to stay where we are.
Now we have to determine whose advice we will take respecting this all important matter, whether we will adhere to Mr.
Clay and his slave holding party, who have always been our
oppressors and murderers, and who are for colonizing us,
more through apprehension than humanity, or to this godly
man who has done so much for our benefit, together with the
advice of all the good and wise among us and the whites. Will
any of us leave our homes and go to Africa? I hope not.*
Let them commence their attack upon us as they did on our
brethren in Ohio, driving and beating us from our country,
and my soul for theirs, they will have enough of it. Let no
man of us budge one step, and let slave-holders come to beat
us from our country. America is more our country, than it is
the whites—we have enriched it with our *blood and tears*.
The greatest riches in all America have arisen from our
blood and tears:—and will they drive us from our property
and homes, which we have earned with our *blood?* They
must look sharp or this very thing will bring swift destruction upon them. The Americans have got so fat on our blood
and groans, that they have almost forgotten the God of
armies. But let them go on.

ADDITION.—I will give here a very imperfect list of the
cruelties inflicted on us by the enlightened Christians of
America.—First, no trifling portion of them will beat us

* Those who are ignorant enough to go to Africa, the coloured people
ought to be glad to have them go, for if they are ignorant enough to let
the whites *fool* them off to Africa, they would be no small injury to us if
they reside in this country.

nearly to death, if they find us on our knees praying to God, —They hinder us from going to hear the word of God—they keep us sunk in ignorance, and will not let us learn to read the word of God, nor write—If they find us with a book of any description in our hand, they will beat us nearly to death—they are so afraid we will learn to read, and enlighten our dark and benighted minds—They will not suffer us to meet together to worship the God who made us—they brand us with hot iron—they cram bolts of fire down our throats— they cut us as they do horses, bulls, or hogs—they crop our ears and sometimes cut off bits of our tongues—they chain and hand-cuff us, and while in that miserable and wretched condition, beat us with cow-hides and clubs—they keep us half naked and starve us sometimes nearly to death under their infernal whips or lashes (which some of them shall have enough of yet)—They put on us fifty-sixes and chains, and make us work in that cruel situation, and in sickness, under lashes to support them and their families.—They keep us three or four hundred feet under ground working in their mines, night and day to dig up gold and silver to enrich them and their children.—They keep us in the most death-like ignorance by keeping us from all source of information, and call us, who are free men and next to the Angels of God, their property!!!!!! They make us fight and murder each other, many of us being ignorant, not knowing any better.— They take us, (being ignorant,) and put us as drivers one over the other, and make us afflict each other as bad as they themselves afflict us—and to crown the whole of this catalogue of cruelties, they tell us that we the (blacks) are an inferior race of beings! incapable of self government!!—We would be injurious to society and ourselves, if tyrants should loose their unjust hold on us!!! That if we were free we would not work, but would live on plunder or theft!!!! that we are the meanest and laziest set of beings in the world!!!!! That they are obliged to keep us in bondage to do us good!!!!!!— That we are satisfied to rest in slavery to them and their children!!!!!!—That we ought not to be set free in America, but ought to be sent away to Africa!!!!!!!!—That if we were set free in America, we would involve the country in a civil war, which assertion is altogether at variance with our feeling or design, for we ask them for nothing but the rights of man, viz. for them to set us free, and treat us like men, and there will be no danger, for we will love and respect them, and protect our country—but cannot conscientiously do these things until they treat us like men.

How cunning slave-holders think they are!!!—How much like the king of Egypt who, after he saw plainly that God was determined to bring out his people, in spite of him and his, as powerful as they were. He was willing that Moses, Aaron and the Elders of Israel, but not all the people should go and serve the Lord. But God deceived him as he will Christian Americans, unless they are very cautious how they move. What would have become of the United States of America, was it not for those among the whites, who not in words barely, but in truth and in deed, love and fear the Lord?—Our Lord and Master said:—*"Whoso shall offend one of these little ones which believe in me, it were better for him that a millstone were hanged about his neck, and that he were drowned in the depth of the sea."

But the Americans with this very threatening of the Lord's, not only beat his little ones among the Africans, but many of them they put to death or murder. Now the avaricious Americans, think that the Lord Jesus Christ will let them off, because his words are no more than the words of a man!!! In fact, many of them are so avaricious and ignorant, that they do not believe in our Lord and Saviour Jesus Christ. Tyrants may think they are so skillful in State affairs is the reason that the government is preserved. But I tell you, that this country woud have been given up long ago, was it not for the lovers of the Lord. They are indeed, the salt of the earth. Remove the people of God among the whites, from this land of blood, and it will stand until they cleverly get out of the way.

* See St. Matthew's Gospel, chap. xviii. 6.

I adopt the language of the Rev. Mr. S. E. Cornish, of New York, editor of the Rights of All, and say: "Any coloured man of common intelligence, who gives his countenance and influence to that colony, further than its missionary object and interest extend, should be considered as a traitor to his brethren, and discarded by every respectable man of colour. And every member of that society, however pure his motive, whatever may be his religious character and moral worth, should in his efforts to remove the coloured population from their rightful soil, the land of their birth and nativity, be considered as acting gratuitously unrighteous and cruel."

Let me make an appeal brethren, to your hearts, for your cordial co-operation in the circulation of "The Rights of All," among us. The utility of such a vehicle if rightly conducted, cannot be estimated. I hope that the well informed among us, may see the absolute necessity of their co-operation in its universal spread among us. If we should let it go down, never let us undertake any thing of the kind again, but give up at once and say that we are really so ignorant and wretched that we cannot do any thing at all!!—As far as I have seen the writings of its editor, I believe he is not seeking to fill his pockets with money, but has the welfare of his brethren truly at heart. Such men, brethren, ought to be supported by us.

But to return to the colonizing trick. It will be well for me to notice here at once, that I do not mean indiscriminately to condemn all the members and advocates of this scheme, for I believe that there are some friends to the sons of Africa, who are laboring for our salvation, not in words only but in truth and in deed, who have been drawn into this plan.— Some, more by persuasion than any thing else; while others, with humane feelings and lively zeal for our good, seeing how much we suffer from the afflictions poured upon us by unmerciful tyrants, are willing to enroll their names in any thing which they think has for its ultimate end our redemption from wretchedness and miseries; such men, with a heart truly overflowing with gratitude for their past services and zeal in our cause, I humbly beg to examine this plot minutely, and see if the end which they have in view will be completely consummated by such a course of procedure. Our friends who have been imperceptibly drawn into this plot I view with tenderness, and would not for the world injure their feelings, and I have only to hope for the future, that they will withdraw themselves from it;—for I declare to them, that the plot is not for the glory of God, but on the contrary the perpetuation of slavery in this country, which will ruin them and the country forever, unless something is immediately done.

Do the colonizationists think to send us off without first being reconciled to us? Do they think to bundle us up like brutes and send us off, as they did our brethren of the State of Ohio?* Have they not to be reconciled to us, or reconcile us to them, for the cruelties with which they have afflicted our fathers and us? Methinks colonizationists think they have a set of brutes to deal with, sure enough. Do they think to drive us from our country and homes, after having enriched it with our blood and tears, and keep back millions of our dear brethren, sunk in the most barbarous wretchedness, to dig up gold and silver for them and their children? Surely, the Americans must think that we are brutes, as some of them have represented us to be. They think that we do not feel for our brethren, whom they are murdering by the inches, but they are dreadfully deceived.

I acknowledge that there are some deceitful and hypocritical wretches among us, who will tell us one thing while

---

* The great slave holder, Mr. John Randolph, of Virginia, intimated in one of his *great, happy* and *eloquent* HARRANGUES, before the Virginia Convention, that Ohio is a slave State, by ranking it among other Slaveholding States. This probably was done by the HONORABLE Slave-holder to deter the minds of the ignorant; to such I would say, that Ohio always was and is now a free State, that it never was and I do not believe it ever will be a Slave-holding State; the people I believe, though some of them are hard hearted enough, detest Slavery too much to admit an evil into their bosom, which gnaws into the very vitals, and sinews of those who are now in possession of it.

they mean another, and thus they go on aiding our enemies to oppress themselves and us. But I declare this day before my Lord and Master, that I believe there are some true-hearted sons of Africa, in this land of oppression, but pretended *liberty*!!!!!—who do in reality feel for their suffering brethren, who are held in bondage by tyrants. Some of the advocates of this cunningly devised plot of Satan represent us to be the greatest set of cut-throats in the world, as though God wants us to take his work out of his hand before he is ready. Does not vengeance belong to the Lord? Is he not able to repay the Americans for their cruelties, with which they have afflicted Africa's sons and daughters, without our interference, unless we are ordered?

It is surprising to think that the Americans, having the Bible in their hands, do not believe it. Are not the hearts of all men in the hands of the God of battles? And does he not suffer some, in consequence of cruelties, to go on until they are irrecoverably lost? Now, what can be more aggravating, than for the Americans, after having treated us so bad, to hold us up to the world as such great throat-cutters? It appears to me as though they are resolved to assail us with every species of affliction that their ingenuity can invent. See the African Repository and Colonial Journal, from its commencement to the present day—see how we are through the medium of that periodical, abused and held up by the Americans, as the greatest nuisance to society, and throat-cutters in the world. But the Lord sees their actions.

Americans! notwithstanding you have and do continue to treat us more cruel than any heathen nation ever did a people it had subjected to the same condition that you have us. Now let us reason—I mean you of the United States, whom I believe God designs to save from destruction, if you will hear. For I declare to you, whether you believe it or not, that there are some on the continent of America, who will never be able to repent. God will surely destroy them, to show you his disapprobation of the murders they and you have inflicted on us. I say, let us reason; had you not better take our body, while you have it in your power, and while we are yet ignorant and wretched, not knowing but a little, give us education, and teach us the pure religion of our Lord and Master, which is calculated to make the lion lay down in peace with the lamb, and which millions of you have beaten us nearly to death for trying to obtain since we have been among you, and thus at once, gain our affection while we are ignorant? Remember Americans, that we must and shall be free and enlightened as you are, will you wait until we shall, under God, obtain our liberty by the crushing arm of power? Will it not be dreadful for you? I speak Americans for your good. We must and shall be free I say, in spite of you. You may do your best to keep us in wretchedness and misery, to enrich you and your children, but God will deliver us from under you. And wo, wo, will be to you if we have to obtain our freedom by fighting. Throw away your fears and prejudices then, and enlighten us and treat us like men, and we will like you more than we do now hate you,* and tell us now no more about colonization, for America is as much our country, as it is yours.—

Treat us like men, and there is no danger but we will all live in peace and happiness together. For we are not like you, hard hearted, unmerciful, and unforgiving. What a happy country this will be, if the whites will listen. What nation under heaven, will be able to do any thing with us, unless God gives us up into its hand? But Americans, I declare to you, while you keep us and our children in bondage, and treat us like brutes, to make us support you and your families, we cannot be your friends. You do not look for it, do you? Treat us then like men, and we will be your friends. And there is not a doubt in my mind, but that the whole of the past will be sunk into oblivion, and we yet, under God, will become a united and happy people. The whites may say it is impossible, but remember that nothing is impossible with God.

* You are not astonished at my saying we hate you, for if we are men, we cannot but hate you, while you are treating us like dogs.

The Americans may say or do as they please, but they have to raise us from the condition of brutes to that of respectable men, and to make a national acknowledgement to us for the wrongs they have inflicted on us. As unexpected, strange, and wild as these propositions may to some appear, it is no less a fact, that unless they are complied with, the Americans of the United States, though they may for a little while escape, God will yet weigh them in a balance, and if they are not superior to other men, as they have represented themselves to be, he will give them wretchedness to their very heart's content.

And now brethren, having concluded these four Articles, I submit them, together with my Preamble, dedicated to the Lord, for your inspection, in language so very simple, that the most ignorant, who can read at all, may easily understand—of which you may make the best you possible can.* Should tyrants take it into their heads to emancipate any of you, remember that your freedom is your natural right. You are men, as well as they, and instead of returning thanks to them for your freedom, return it to the Holy Ghost, who is our rightful owner. If they do not want to part with your labours, which have enriched them, let them keep you, and my word for it, that God Almighty, will break their strong

* Some of my brethren, who are sensible, do not take an interest in enlightening the minds of our more ignorant brethren respecting this BOOK, and in reading it to them, just as though they will not have either to stand or fall by what is written in this book. Do they believe that I would be so foolish as to put out a book of this kind without strict—ah! very strict commandments of the Lord?—Surely the blacks and whites must think that I am ignorant enough.—Do they think that I would have the audacious wickedness to take the name of my God in vain?

Notice, I said in the concluding clause of Article 3—I call God, I call Angels, I call men to witness, that the destruction of the Americans is at hand, and will be speedily consummated unless they repent. Now I wonder if the world think that I would take the name of God in this way in vain? What do they think I take God to be? Do they suppose that I would trifle with that God who will not have his Holy name taken in vain?—He will show you and the world, in due time, whether this book is for his glory, or written by me through envy to the whites, as some have represented.

band. Do you believe this, my brethren?—See my Address, delivered before the General Coloured Association of Massachusetts, which may be found in Freedom's Journal, for Dec. 20, 1828.—See the last clause of that Address. Whether you believe it or not, I tell you that God will dash tyrants, in combination with devils, into atoms, and will bring you out from your wretchedness and miseries under these *Christian People*!!!!!!

Those philanthropists and lovers of the human family, who have volunteered their services for our redemption from wretchedness, have a high claim on our gratitude, and we should always view them as our greatest earthly benefactors.

If any are anxious to ascertain who I am, know the world, that I am one of the oppressed, degraded and wretched sons of Africa, rendered so by the avaricious and unmerciful, among the whites.—If any wish to plunge me into the wretched incapacity of a slave, or murder me for the truth, know ye, that I am in the hand of God, and at your disposal. I count my life not dear unto me, but I am ready to be offered at any moment. For what is the use of living, when in fact I am dead. But remember, Americans, that as miserable, wretched, degraded and abject as you have made us in preceding, and in this generation, to support you and your families, that some of you, (whites) on the continent of America, will yet curse the day that you ever were born. You want slaves, and want us for your slaves!!! My colour will yet, root some of you out of the very face of the earth!!!!!! You may doubt it if you please. I know that thousands will doubt—they think they have us so well secured in wretchedness, to them and their children, that it is impossible for such things to occur.* So did the antideluvians doubt Noah, until

* Why do the Slave-holders or Tyrants of America and their advocates fight so hard to keep my brethren from receiving and reading my Book of Appeal to them?—Is it because they treat us so well?—Is it because we are satisfied to rest in Slavery to them and their children?—Is it because they are treating us like men, by compensating us all over this free country!! for our labours?—But why are the Americans so very fearfully terrified respecting

the day in which the flood came and swept them away. So did the Sodomites doubt, until Lot had got out of the city, and

my Book?—Why do they search vessels, &c. when entering the harbours of tyrannical States, to see if any of my Books can be found, for fear that my brethren will get them to read. Why, I thought the Americans proclaimed to the world that they are a happy, enlightened, humane and Christian people all the inhabitants of the country enjoy equal Rights!! America is the Asylum for the oppressed of all nations!!!

Now I ask the Americans to see the fearful terror they labor under for fear that my brethren will get my Book and read it and tell me if their declaration is true—viz. if the United States of America is a Republican Government?—Is this not the most tyrannical, unmerciful, and cruel government under Heaven—not excepting the Algerines, Turks and Arabs?—I believe if any candid person would take the trouble to go through the Southern and Western sections of this country, and could have the heart to see the cruelties inflicted by these *Christians* on us, he would say, that the Algerines, Turks and Arabs treat their dogs a thousand times better than we are treated by the *Christians*.—But perhaps the Americans do their very best to keep my Brethren from receiving and reading my "Appeal" for fear they will find in it an extract which I made from their Declaration of Independence, which says, "we hold these truths to be self-evident, that all men are created equal," &c. &c. &c.—If the above are not the causes of the alarm among the Americans, respecting my Book, I do not know what to impute it to, unless they are possessed of the same spirit with which Demetrius the Silversmith was possessed—however, that they may judge whether they are of the same avaricious and ungodly spirit with that man, I will give here an extract from the Acts of the Apostles, chapter xix.—verses 23, 24, 25, 26, 27.

"And the same time there arose no small stir about that way. For a certain *man* named Demetrius, a silversmith, which made silver shrines for Diana, brought no small gain unto the craftsmen; whom he called together with the workmen of like occupation, and said, Sirs, ye know that by this craft we have our wealth: moreover, ye see and hear, that not alone at Ephesus, but almost throughout all Asia, this Paul hath persuaded and turned away much people, saying, that they be no gods which are made with hands: so that not only this our craft is in danger to be set at nought; but also that the temple of the great goddess Diana should be despised, and her magnificence should be destroyed, whom all Asia and the world worshippeth."

I pray you Americans of North and South America, together with the whole European inhabitants of the world, (I mean Slave-holders and their advocates) to read and ponder over the above verses in your minds, and judge whether or not you are of the infernal spirit with that Heathen Demetrius, the Silversmith: In fine I beg you to read the whole chapter through carefully.

140

God rained down fire and brimstone from Heaven upon them, and burnt them up. So did the king of Egypt doubt the very existence of a God; he said, "who is the Lord, that I should let Israel go?" Did he not find to his sorrow, who the Lord was, when he and all his mighty men of war, were smothered to death in the Red Sea? So did the Romans doubt, many of them were really so ignorant, that they thought the whole of mankind were made to be slaves to them; just as many of the Americans think now, of my colour. But they got dreadfully deceived. When men got their eyes opened, they made the murderers scamper. The way in which they cut their tyrannical throats, was not much inferior to the way the Romans or murderers, served them, when they held them wretchedness and degradation under their feet. So would Christian Americans doubt, if God should send an Angel from Heaven to preach their funeral sermon. The fact is, the Christians having a name to live, while they are dead, think that God will screen them on that ground.

See the hundreds and thousands of us that are thrown into the seas by Christians, and murdered by them in other ways. They cram us into their vessel holds in chains and in hand-cuffs—men, women and children, all together!! O! save us, we pray thee, thou God of Heaven and of earth, from the devouring hands of the white Christians!!!

Oh! thou Alpha and Omega!
The beginning and the end,
Enthron'd thou art in Heaven above,
Surrounded by Angels there:

From whence thou seest the miseries
To which we are subject;
The whites have murder'd us, O God!
And kept us ignorant of thee.

Not satisfied with this, my Lord!
They throw us in the seas:
Be pleas'd, we pray, for Jesus' sake,
To save us from their grasp.

We believe that, for thy glory's sake,
Thou wilt deliver us;
But that thou may'st effect these things,
Thy glory must be sought.

In conclusion, I ask the candid and unprejudiced of the whole world, to search the pages of historians diligently, and see if the Antideluvians—the Sodomites—the Egyptians—the Babylonians—the Ninevites—the Carthagenians—the Persians—the Macedonians—the Greeks—the Romans—the Mahometans—the Jews—or devils, ever treated a set of human beings, as the white Christians of America do us, the blacks, or Africans. I also ask the attention of the world of mankind to the declaration of these very American people, of the United States.

A declaration made July 4, 1776.

It says,

    * When in the course of human events, it becomes necessary for one people to dissolve the political bands which have connected them with another, and to assume among the Powers of the earth, the separate and equal station to which the laws of nature and of nature's God entitle them. A decent respect for the opinions of mankind requires, that they should declare the causes which impel them to the separation.—We hold these truths to be self evident—that all men are created equal, that they are endowed by their Creator with certain unalienable rights: that among these, are life, liberty, and the pursuit of happiness that, to secure these rights, governments are instituted among men, deriving their just powers from the consent of the governed; that when ever any form of government becomes destructive of these ends, it is the right of the people to alter or to abolish it, and to institute a new government laying its foundation on such principles, and organizing its powers in such form, as to them shall

* See the Declaration of Independence of the United States.

142

seem most likely to effect their safety and happiness. Prudence, indeed, will dictate, that governments long established should not be changed for light and transient causes; and accordingly all experience hath shewn, that mankind are more disposed to suffer, while evils are sufferable, than to right themselves by abolishing the forms to which they are accustomed. But when a long train of abuses and usurpations, pursuing invariably the same object, envinces a design to reduce them under absolute despotism, it is their right it is their duty to throw off such government, and to provide new guards for their future security.

See your Declaration Americans!!! Do you understand your own language? Hear your language, proclaimed to the world, July 4th, 1776—

We hold these truths to be self evident—that ALL men are created EQUAL!! that they *are endowed by their creator with certain unalienable rights;* that among these are life, *liberty,* and the pursuit of happiness!!

Compare your own language above, extracted from your Declaration of Independence, with your cruelties and murders inflicted by your cruel and unmerciful fathers and yourselves on our fathers and on us—men who have never given your fathers or you the least provocation!!!!!!

Hear your language further!

But when a long train of abuses and usurpation, pursuing invariably the same object, evinces a design to reduce them under absolute despotism, it is their *right,* it is their *duty,* to throw off such government, and to provide new guards for their future security.

Now, Americans! I ask you candidly, was your sufferings under Great Britain, one hundredth part as cruel and tyrannical as you have rendered ours under you? Some of you, no doubt, believe that we will never throw off your murderous government and "provide new guards for our future security." If Satan has made you believe it, will he not deceive you?* Do the whites say, I being a black man, ought to be humble, which I readily admit? I ask them, ought they not to be as humble as I? or do they think that they can measure arms with Jehovah? Will not the Lord yet humble them? or will not these very coloured people whom they now treat worse than brutes, yet under God, humble them low down enough? Some of the whites are ignorant enough to tell us, that we ought to be submissive to them that they may keep their feet on our throats. And if we do not submit to be beaten to death by them, we are bad creatures and of course must be damned, &c.

If any man wishes to hear this doctrine openly preached to us by the American preachers, let him go into the Southern and Western sections of this country—I do not speak from hear say—what I have written, is what I have seen and heard myself. No man may think that my book is made up of conjecture—I have travelled and observed nearly the whole of those things myself, and what little I did not get by my own observation, I received from those among the whites and blacks, in whom the greatest confidence may be placed.

The Americans may be as vigilant as they please, but they cannot be vigilant enough for the Lord, neither can they hide themselves, where he will not find and bring them out.

> 1 Thy presence why withdraw'st, Lord?
>   Why hid'st thou now thy face,
>   When dismal times of deep distress
>   Call for thy wonted grace?
>
> 2 The wicked, swell'd with lawless pride,
>   Have made the poor their prey;
>   O let them fall by those designs
>   Which they for others lay.

---

* The Lord has not taught the Americans that we will not some day or other throw off their chains and hand-cuffs from our hands and feet, and their devilish lashes (which some of them shall have enough of yet) from off our backs.

3 For straight they triumph, if success
　　Their thriving crimes attend;
　And sordid wretches, whom God hates,
　　Perversely they command.

4 To own a pow'r above themselves
　　Their haughty pride disdains;
　And, therefore, in their stubborn mind
　　No thought of God remains.

5 Oppressive methods they pursue,
　　And all their foes they slight;
　Because thy judgments, unobserv'd,
　　Are far above their sight.

6 They fondly think their prosp'rous state
　　Shall unmolested be;
　They think their vain designed shall thrive,
　　From all misfortune free.

7 Vain and deceitful is their speech,
　　With curses fill'd, and lies;
　By which the mischief of their heart
　　They study to disguise.

8 Near public roads they lie conceal'd
　　And all their art employ,
　The innocent and poor at once
　　To rifle and destroy.

9 Not lions, crouching in their dens,
　　Surprise their heedless prey
　With greater cunning, or express
　　More savage rage than they.

10 Sometimes they act the harmless man,
　　And modest looks they wear;
　That so, deceiv'd the poor may less
　　Their sudden onset fear.

PART II.

11 For, God, they think, no notice takes,
    Of their unrighteous deeds;
  He never minds the suff'ring poor,
    Nor their oppression heeds.

12 But thou, O Lord, at length arise,
    Stretch forth thy mighty arm,
  And, by the greatness of thy pow'r,
    Defend the poor from harm.

13 No longer let the wicked vaunt,
    And, proudly boasting, say,
  "Tush, God regards not what we do;
    "He never will repay."—*Common Prayer Book.*

1 Shall I for fear of feeble man,
    The spirit's course in me restrain?
  Or, undismay'd in deed and word,
    Be a true witness of my Lord.

2 Aw'd by mortal's frown, shall I
    Conceal the word of God Most High!
  How then before thee shall I dare
    To stand, or how thy anger bear?

3 Shall I, to soothe th' unholy thong,
    Soften the truth, or smooth my tongue,
  To gain earth's gilded toys or, flee
    The cross endur'd, my Lord, by thee?

4 What then is he whose scorn I dread?
    Whose wrath or hate makes me afraid
  A man! an heir of death! a slave
    To sin! a bubble on the wave!

5 Yea, let men rage, since thou will spread
    Thy shadowing wings around my head:

146

Since in all pain thy tender love
Will still my sure refreshment prove.

Wesleys Collection.

It may not be understood, when I say my Third and last Edition, I mean to convey the idea, that there will be no more Books of this Third Edition printed, but to notify that there will be no more addition in the body of this Work, or additional Notes to this "Appeal."

THE END

VIII: BIBLIOGRAPHY

Adams, Alice D.: *The Neglected Period of Anti-Slavery in America (1808-1831)* (Boston, 1908, Ginn & Co.)

Aptheker, Herbert; *American Negro Slave Revolts* (N.Y., 1943, Columbia Univ., Press; N.Y., 1963, International Publishers)

——: *Essays in the History of the American Negro* (N.Y., 1945, International Pub.)

——: *To be Free: Studies in Negro History* (N.Y., 1948, International Pub.)

——: *A Documentary History of the Negro People in the United States* (N.Y., 1951, Citadel Press)

Bell, H. H.: "Expressions of Negro Militancy in the North, 1840-1860," in *The Journal of Negro History*, January, 1960

Brawley, Benjamin: *A Social History of the American Negro* (N.Y., 1921, Macmillan)

Brewer, W. M.: "Henry Highland Garnet," in *The Journal of Negro History*, January, 1928

Carroll, J. C., *Slave Insurrections in the U.S.* (Boston, 1938, Chapman & Grimes)

Chapman, John Jay: *William Lloyd Garrison* (N.Y., 1913, Moffat, Yard)

Curti, Merle: *The Learned Blacksmith, The Life and Journals of Elihu Burritt* (N.Y., 1937, Univ. of Wisconsin Press)

Du Bois, W. E. B.: *The Suppression of the African Slave-Trade to the United States of America, 1638-1870* (Cambridge, 1896, Harvard Univ. Press; see also the 1954 edition, issued by The Social Science Press, N. Y.)

Dumond, Dwight L.: *Antislavery: The Crusade for Freedom in America* (Ann Arbor, 1961, Univ. of Michigan Press)

Eaton, Clement: "A Dangerous Pamphlet in the Old South," in *The Journal of Southern History*, August, 1936

——: *Freedom of Thought in the Old South* (Durham, 1940, Duke Univ. Press)

Filler, Louis: *The Crusade Against Slavery 1830-1860* (N.Y., 1960, Harper)

Franklin, John H.: "Slaves Virtually Free in Ante-Bellum North Carolina," in *The Journal of Negro History,* July, 1943

——: *From Slavery to Freedom: A History of American Negroes* (N.Y., 1947, Knopf)

[Garrison, W. P. & F. J.]: *William Lloyd Garrison 1805-1879. The Story of his Life, told by his children* (N.Y., 1885, Century, Vol. I)

Gross, Bella: "Freedom's Journal and the Rights of All," in *The Journal of Negro History,* July, 1932

Gruening, Martha: "David Walker," in *The Dictionary of American Biography,* Vol. XIX, p. 340 (N.Y., 1943, Scribner's)

Lader, Lawrence: *The Bold Brahmins: New England's War Against Slavery, 1831-1863* (N.Y., 1961, Dutton)

Litwack, Leon F.: *North of Slavery: The Negro in the Free States, 1790-1860* (Chicago, 1961, Univ. of Chicago Press)

Loggins, Vernon: *The Negro Author: His Development in America* (N.Y., 1931, Columbia Univ. Press)

May, S. J.: *Some Recollections of the Anti-Slavery Conflict* (Boston, 1869, Field, Osgood)

Nye, R. B.: *Fettered Freedom: Civil Liberties and the Slavery Controversy 1830-1860* (East Lansing, 1949, Michigan State Univ. Press)

Redding, J. Saunders: *They Came in Chains: Americans from Africa* (Phila., N.Y., 1950, Lippincott)

Staudenraus, P. J.: *The African Colonization Movement, 1816-1865* (N.Y., 1961, Columbia Univ. Press)

Warner, R. A.: *New Haven Negroes* (New Haven, 1940, Yale Univ. Press)

Wesley, Charles H.: *Richard Allen* (Washington, 1937, Associated Pub.)

Woodson, Carter G.: *The History of the Negro Church* (Washington, 1921, Associated Pub.)

—— ed.: *The Mind of the Negro as reflected in letters written during the crisis, 1800-1860* (Washington, 1926, Associated Pub.)